Lighted Windows

Advent Reflections for a World in Waiting

MARGARET SILF

UPPER ROOM BOOKS®
NASHVILLE

Cover illustration: Sherry Neidigh
Cover design: TMW Designs
Interior design: Gore Studio, Inc. / www.GoreStudio.com
First printing: 2004
First published in 2002 by The Bible Reading Fellowship, 15–17 Elsfield Way, Oxford OX2 8FG

Library of Congress Cataloging-in-Publication Data
Silf, Margaret.
    Lighted windows : Advent reflections for a world in waiting / Margaret Silf.
        p. cm.
    Originally published: Oxford : Bible Reading Fellowship, 2002.
    ISBN 0-8358-9886-5
1. Advent—Meditations. 2. Epiphany—Meditations. I. Title.
    BV40.S55 2004
    242'.332—dc22   2004002627

Printed in the United States of America

Praise for *Lighted Windows*

Margaret Silf has done something unusual and delightful for me in this book: she has helped me look at some familiar passages of scripture in new ways. Many of the texts she has chosen are not ones we usually associate with the waiting days of Advent, which enriches reflection. Silf's writing style is readable and her questions insightful, and the short length of the meditations makes them inviting and practical for the busy days of Advent. Those who keep spiritual journals will find ample spurs for their writing in Silf's continual connections of daily life with the truth and questions of the Advent story.

— MARY LOU REDDING
Managing Editor, *The Upper Room* daily devotional guide
Author of *While We Wait: Living the Questions of Advent*

Lighted Windows is an Advent blessing, providing deep, daily self-examination in the light of scripture. Silf writes with insight that places her reader right into the sandals of Bible personalities such as Elizabeth, John the Baptist, Mary of Nazareth, Rhoda, and the Magi. In many chapters *Lighted Windows* challenges us to truly open our hearts not only to the baby born in Bethlehem but also to his friends: those people living on the fringes—the poor, the sick, the imprisoned. Best of all, Silf maintains focus on the central reason for the faith—not dogma, creed, liturgy, sermon, or even scripture, but rather that unmistakable feeling in the individual human heart once it has felt the touch of the Almighty, the personal reality of the message of Advent and Christmas: Emmanuel—God with us.

—Jim Melchiorre
Author of *Reflections of Messiah*
Television journalist and producer

Contents

Introduction

THE FIRST OF DECEMBER, and Christmas is just around the corner! It's the season of expectation, of hope, of anticipation. A season of dreams, and for Christians, a season where the deepest dream of all humankind meets face-to-face with God's own dream for God's creation, made visible and tangible to everyone who seeks.

One of my most abiding memories is of an evening shared with a friend who had experienced a particularly traumatic childhood. We were talking about our favorite fairy tales, and she told me, with tears in her eyes, of how much the story of "The Little Matchgirl" had come to mean for her, not just in her dreams but in her Christian journeying too.

"The Little Matchgirl" wasn't a story I was familiar with, but as she retold it, it came to life in a way that reflects, for me, something of the spirit of this Advent journey. The little matchgirl was a young child, undernourished and very poor. She earned her daily bread by selling matches, but the earnings were sparse, and at home a cruel father waited to punish her if she failed to bring home enough money. One dark winter night she was standing in her usual place, shivering and gazing at the lighted windows of the big houses all around her, catching fleeting glimpses of all that was going on inside those rooms—the preparations for Christmas, the lovely gifts, the bright decorations, the happy faces, the smell of Christmas puddings and roasting goose.

All she had was a box of matches, and there were no customers tonight—they all had other things on their minds. *Dare I strike one?* she wondered. She took out a match and struck it, gazing for a few brief moments into its blaze of light. As she did so, she imagined that it was one of those lighted windows. She looked inside, in her imagination, and entered into a warm room where loving friends might welcome her. Another match, another scene. Another window to look into. Perhaps a fine dinner set out for a family. The crackling of the goose, the aroma of mince pies. Food and shelter. And so she continued, until she came to the last match in the box.

The story has a bittersweet ending. As she strikes her last match, the little matchgirl sees a shooting star falling across the night sky, and her granny is standing there, smiling, waiting to gather the child into her arms and carry her home to heaven. The frozen child is discovered the next morning with an empty matchbox in her hands and a deep, contented smile across her white face.

This Advent journey invites you to share something of the magic and the mystery of what it means to look into some of your own "lighted windows." But these are not the windows of fantasy. They are the windows of our common quest to discover "God-with-us"—Emmanuel, God incarnate in the world of everyday reality with all its shame and its glory. They are like the windows of an Advent calendar, leading us ever closer to the mystery that is born in Bethlehem.

During the first three weeks of the journey, we look, day by day, into a series of windows opening up into glimpses of how we might discover God's guidance in our lives, how we might become more trusting of that guidance, and how we might catch something of God's wisdom.

During Christmas week, the windows open wide, inviting us to enter right into the heart of the mystery of God's coming to earth.

And as the journey moves on to the turning of the year and the feast of the Epiphany, the windows turn into doors, through which we are sent out again into a world that is waiting—and longing—for the touch of God's love upon its broken heart.

The child who comes to us in Bethlehem is also cradled in bittersweetness, like the child in the story. The starlight will turn into the interrogator's beam; the straw will become a crown of thorns. Yet this will be the eye of the needle that will open into a wholeness and completeness that our earthbound hearts and minds cannot begin to imagine.

Each day's reflection includes an invitation to look into its "window" in a way that connects the God-story with your story and your circumstances in a personal way—a way that makes a difference—so that God-with-us becomes ever more authentically God-with-you.

May your journey be blessed and joyful, and may it lead you daily more deeply into who you truly are—the person God dreamed you to be when God created you.

———⚉———

Glimpses
of Guidance

MOST OF US find ourselves wishing from time to time that some-one would show us the way. During the next few days, we look at some of the ways in which guidance is given and how we react to it.

We begin and end this part of the Advent journey with John the Baptist—a man who allowed God to guide him and who became a guide to others. As the days go by, we pause to reflect on how God's guidance is to be found in:

- the call to take risks (December 1)
- the tendency of God to break right through our careful planning (December 2)
- the touch of God when we are in the pits of despair (December 3)
- the leading of God through our life's mazes (December 4)
- the challenge to go beyond set "answers" (December 5)
- the choices we make, moment by moment (December 6)
- the signposts we discover that point beyond themselves to God (December 7)

Risks

—— ∞∞∞ ——

Read Luke 1:11-24, 57-64.

If only God would write instructions across the sky, we might often be tempted to think. If only it were obvious what we should do, which direction we should choose, how we should react to a particular person or situation. But life rarely gives us that kind of certainty. More often our choices and decisions are full of ambiguity and mixed motivation, and the best we can hope for is to do a minimum of harm—a goal far removed from the desire that burns in our hearts to live true to the very best of our visions.

Perhaps, as the years go by, our attempts to follow the path of God, however we envision it, may become like Zechariah's—refined but also reduced to the faithful fulfillment of a set of obligations and the leading of what might pass as a good life. Such faithfulness is never to be despised. It can be the seedbed of God's kingdom. Unfortunately, it can all too easily turn into a comfort zone. We feel so settled in our holy niche that we stop even expecting God to intervene in our lives. We carry on "burning our incense." We keep on tending that flickering little fire within us that still burns with a love for God. But we don't expect to wake up one morning and discover that the flames are suddenly leaping out of control. Neither did Zechariah!

In short, our waiting upon God can become simply the habit of waiting for its own sake—like waiting day after day in line at the bus stop but being wholly unprepared for the possibility that the bus might actually arrive. So stunned are we when the bus turns up that we step back in disbelief and refuse to get on board. How do we know that the bus isn't some figment of our imagination? How do we know that this is really our bus and that it will take us to where we want to be? What if we can't pay the fare? What if it all turns out to be too costly? Maybe it would be just so much easier, and safer, to stay in line at the bus stop. After all, we know where we are when we're standing at the bus stop. Who knows where we might end up if we get on the bus?

We might imagine Zechariah going through a similar thought process. His faithful, lifelong prayers for God's guidance are suddenly answered, and he doesn't know how to respond. His coping mechanism is to try to interpret the divine touch of God in terms of merely human logic: *This doesn't make sense within my terms of reference, so I will dismiss it.* But God's touch, as we know from experience, confounds human logic and goes far beyond it. Often, the best, most visionary things we do in life are fueled not by reason and logic but by intuition, imagination, and desire.

Zechariah's story encourages me. It reminds me I'm not the only one to fail to recognize God's guidance even when it is given to me on a plate, and that however stubbornly I fail to respond, God's purposes will not be deflected. Elizabeth's child is going to come into the world, whatever his father may think about the possibility. It is Zechariah, and not God, who is disempowered by his refusal to respond to the guidance he is being given.

I am encouraged too by the fact that the disempowerment was not permanent. Just as the infant John would need nine months' gestation before coming to birth, so Zechariah is also given a time of gestation in which his response can grow and ripen into the wholehearted "Yes!" expressed in the moment when he writes on the tablet, "His name is John."

God will wait for our response. And God will wait for as long as it takes.

14

"How will I know that this is so?"

When you got up this morning, you had no idea what the day would bring. But you probably chose to take a chance on it and not go back to bed. God invites us to take a chance on life too, without knowing where God's guidance will lead us. To the extent that we can say "Yes," we will discover the next step along the way. To the extent that we hold back, we will get stuck where we are, until we are ready to move on again. How do you feel about the response you want to make to God in the light of the challenges today will bring?

Lord, I can't see the bright sunlight of your leading because my eyes are focused on the little candle of my own thinking. Blow out the candle if you must, and give me the grace to see your light in my darkness. Amen.

Plans

Read Exodus 3:1-12.

I wonder how many years of my life I have actually spent waiting. I don't mean just those hours waiting in lines or in traffic jams, or on one end of multiple-choice recorded phone messages with no sign of a human being at the other. At times like that, the waiting game is an obvious frustration. No, I am thinking more of all those days I have spent staring out of the office window or at the view from the kitchen sink, thinking to myself that everything will be better when such and such happens. With this kind of mind-set, I have spent literally years and years waiting—waiting for the holidays to come around, for the boss to move on, for the next promotion or the next exam, waiting for children to arrive, waiting for them to grow up and be independent, and then waiting for them to come home again to visit! The grass is quite simply *always* going to be greener around the next bend in the road.

The same kind of logic has shaped my search for God's guidance in my life. I have sat down with God in prayer and laid out my plans before God, pointing out, in ways the Almighty surely couldn't misunderstand, exactly where I needed divine help. Then I have been unpleasantly surprised when that guidance apparently wasn't forthcoming.

Maybe Moses was prey to thoughts like these too, as he tended his father-in-law's flocks at Horeb. He had been forced to flee from justice, having killed an Egyptian who was harassing one of the Israelites—a change of plan he had probably not bargained for. And we find him now looking after the sheep, biding his time and keeping a low profile.

God has other plans. Into the midst of Moses' neat arrangements comes a burning bush! Suddenly he is confronted by something wholly unexpected. Thankfully, for all of us, Moses had enough space in his heart and mind to give God a chance to break through. He had the grace to see the burning bush and to take it seriously. He was willing to put his own plans on hold and, as it were, switch channels to listen to what God was trying to communicate.

What can we learn from this encounter about the pattern of God's guidance? A few thoughts come to mind:

- God's guidance attracts us; it doesn't coerce us.
- It usually takes us by surprise.
- It happens when we are going about our everyday living, and it grows out of that everyday experience, if we have eyes to see.
- It is not destructive, although it sometimes seems as if it will be. We have to cross a threshold of trust if we want to engage with it.
- We have to come close enough to hear it.
- We will recognize it in those moments when we sense that we are on holy ground.
- It may lead us to places we would rather not go.

God's guidance may begin with a peak experience for us, but it is given for the benefit of more than just ourselves. Our God is a relational God—a trinity of Father, Son, and Spirit—and the guidance God gives is not just for ourselves but is to be put into practice in a relational, interdependent world.

"The place on which you are standing is holy ground."

Perhaps you can look back on moments that shaped or reshaped your life. It might be helpful to reflect on these experiences in the light of Moses' encounter with the burning bush. How did you react when you felt God's touch on your life in some powerful way? What guidance was given? How did it tally with your own "planning"? Was it just for you, or did it have wider implications? How did you work it out in practice? Or perhaps you didn't recognize it at all at the time but can only see its outworkings with the benefit of hindsight.

An acquaintance of mine whose life had been recently derailed once said to me, "What makes God laugh? Answer: People who make plans!" Let us not become so entangled in the shaping of our years that we miss the signpost that is standing right here in the present moment.

Lord, please help me to laugh with you about my own so-serious planning, and then let us move on together in the light of your surprises. Amen.

Pits

———◦≈◦———

Read 1 Kings 19:3-13.

It's strangely reassuring to know that the mightiest prophets can also suffer from depression and find themselves drawing a complete blank in their attempt to discover what God is up to. This kind of despair seems to bring down the curtains on all our spiritual journeying. It can stop us in our tracks. We lie down and sink into our own personal dark pit. Like an accident victim on a cold, exposed mountainside, all we want to do is to sink into oblivion. The desire to sleep away our sorrows can lead us to a real risk of spiritual hypothermia, the kind of sleep from which we may never awaken.

This seems to be the mood Elijah is in today. He is wishing he were dead, and telling God how he feels. Perhaps you know the place in your own experience.

So where is God's guidance when we find ourselves at the end of our rope? And what is our chance of finding it, let alone of following it? Maybe this incident from Elijah's story can give us a few clues, as it reveals how God deals with this kind of despair—a pattern just as relevant today as it was in the time of Elijah.

- First God encourages us to express how we feel. Often a listener appears—someone we can trust—possibly not the person we would have expected or even chosen, but someone, nevertheless, and that someone may be our "angel."
- Next (through our "angel") God gives us something, maybe a small something, to boost our positive energy a

bit and to stop us from falling into the sleep of despair. For Elijah it was simple fare—bread and water—but fresh, appetizing, and just enough to revive his spirits.

- Then God waits until we are ready, and when the right moment comes, the Holy One gives us a bit more to strengthen us for the onward journey.

When I look back over the ups and downs of my own life (especially the downs), I can see how this pattern has recurred. The intervention that made a difference has come to me through "angels." The "angels" may have been colleagues, neighbors, or even complete strangers. At the time, I probably didn't recognize the hand of God in their kindness and caring, but with hindsight I can see clearly that these were definitive moments that drew me beyond despair and gave me strength to keep going.

Often such guidance has come gradually, one step at a time, bringing a little more encouragement each time. It isn't a divine Concorde that jets us to the holy mountain, but our own step-by-step response to the angels' encouragement.

But this isn't the end of the waiting. Even at the mountaintop, Elijah is asked to wait, to observe, and to expect the unexpected. In that waiting space, God reveals God's self in ways we don't expect. Not in the spectacular and loud and fear-inspiring, not in the powerful and earthshaking, but in the stillness of our hearts.

In this secret, holy place, we will know when God is close, and we will "cover our faces" in awe. And then, only then, will we hear the instructions for the next step.

"An angel touched him."

Elijah's story gives us a map of the terrain we might be in when we seek God's guidance in a time of despair. Does it connect at all to your own experience of being in this kind of terrain? Who have your angels been? How have they moved you on? What was the "bread and water" that kept you going? What does the holy mountain mean for you? And do these memories help you move more trustfully into the future?

It doesn't have to be some cataclysmic disaster that pitches us into despair. In fact, it's much more likely to be a thoughtless word, an undeserved criticism, a creeping anxiety—the very stuff of everyday life. And the journey to the holy mountain needn't be a huge pilgrimage. It can be as simple as going aside for ten minutes to a quiet place where we can tell God how we feel, just as Elijah did. We can safely leave the rest to God, just as Elijah did.

Out of the depths I call, Lord; in those depths let me meet you. Amen.

DECEMBER 4

Mazes

Read Exodus 13:17-22 and 40:36-38.

I have a basalt "labyrinth stone," formed over six hundred million years ago out of the volcanic turmoil that formed the
Lleyn Peninsula in Wales. Shaped and smoothed by the sea
through all the ages, and now engraved with the symbol of a
labyrinth, this stone has become a prayer stone. It reminds me
that the search for God almost never leads in a straight line and
that it may demand much patient waiting. When I look back
over my life so far, I often want to ask God why on earth we did
not take a quicker, easier route through the various obstacles that
presented themselves. With hindsight it always looks as though
there would have been a more straightforward, less painful and
confusing path.

Labyrinths and mazes are a universal human symbol of the
search for what matters most. There seems to be a deep human
intuition that the convolutions of life are the very places where
we do our growing and our learning. They force us to wait for the
next step to become clear. They lead us into cul-de-sacs and back-
waters, bringing us face-to-face with our human limitations. They
frustrate us and confound our "wisdom." Yet they make up our
path, and there is no other.

Rivers tell us the same kind of story. When they come up to
an obstruction, they find a way to flow around it. No doubt, if a
river could speak, it too would express its frustration at the many
boulders that have blocked its way. But would it also realize how

much more of the barren earth has been visited and watered by its stream in the process?

The Israelites could have taken the coastal road, but God had a hidden agenda. The shortest route would also have provided an easy escape route. How easy to run "back to Egypt" (and to captivity) at the first difficulty, if the road had been straight and obvious. And yes, I too would have run back to base many a time, when faced with problems too hard to solve, if I could have found the way! As it was, I was so embroiled in the twists and turns of my life's journey that the only way forward was to trust in the next step and wait for some kind of clarity to come out of the confusion. And that trusting and waiting, I discover, has been the way God has been guiding me and growing me all along.

It would be a bleak picture indeed if all we had to hope for were a labyrinth of confusion. But more lies in the maze than we might have dared to hope. There is a dream—and a fire.

The Israelites, we learn, carried the bones of Joseph with them on their momentous trek through the desert. Why? Because Joseph was their dreamer, the symbol of their God-dream. So, though we are urged to travel light, we must carry our dream with us, wherever the labyrinth of life may lead us. The dream is our energy for the road. It is our memory of those moments when God has unmistakably touched our lives. It is a sacred space and a still center in all our confusion. We need to return to it regularly to replenish our resources for the way.

While we carry the dream, God can be trusted to provide the fire. For the Israelites, as so often for ourselves, the fire of God's leading seems to be concealed in a cloud of unknowing. Paradoxically, it is in the place where we are unable to find our own way that God is most powerfully present to us. The fire at the heart of the cloud only becomes visible at night, when we are in the darkest stretches of our life's journey.

"And fire was in the cloud."

My labyrinth stone has had to wait for millions of years to discover what it really is. While it was being hurled around in the throes of volcanic activity or battered by the force of the sea, it could never have imagined that one day it would become a pebble that would help lead a human heart closer to God. It teaches me to do my own waiting with an open and expectant heart. What shape is your stone taking?

I have a dream, Lord, and you are the fire. Let us risk the maze of being, hand in hand. Amen.

Answer Books

Read Jeremiah 29:11-14 and 31:33-34.

Perhaps you have heard the story of the schoolboy who dreamed of becoming a mathematician. This fellow also liked to go out on the town in the evenings, and he often skipped his homework. When this happened, he would hastily throw his assignments together on the bus the next morning by looking at the answers at the end of the book.

One day his teacher took him aside and told him a simple truth: "You will never become a mathematician by looking up the answers to the problems in the back of the book," he said, "even though, ironically, those answers will usually be the right ones."

Perhaps this wisdom is part of what lies behind the game of hide-and-seek that God appears to play with us so often. "Come on," the Creator urges us, "come and look for me. Where have I hidden myself today?"

Is this game God's idea of fun? we might be forgiven for wondering. Or is it, rather, God's way of teaching our hearts God's meanings and ways? We might almost hear our Maker whispering gently, "You will never become fully the person I created you to be by plagiarizing life's answers from creeds and doctrines, even though these doctrines may well be right and true. You will only become your true self by working through for yourself the challenges that life presents."

A daunting prospect! But from Jeremiah's words today we discover that we are not alone in the task. God has promised to plant God's law deep within our own hearts. So does this mean that we have some kind of "answer book" inside us, if we only knew how to access it? I think not, much as we might wish it were so! God's answers don't come ready-made. They must be discovered. And the prophet goes on to give us a clue about this process of discovery.

This law that God has planted in our hearts, it seems, is more like the bond of a personal relationship than the terms of an equation. It is a sense of alignment between our own hearts and the heart of God, which will deepen and strengthen every time we use it, so that gradually, step-by-step, we will learn to recognize when we are acting out of our truest center, and when we are slipping off course. The closer we come to this kind of discernment, the less we will need human guides and teachers.

The giving of God's guidance is something organic and alive. The Almighty plants it in our hearts and writes it for each of us uniquely. And then God gives it growth until it bears the fruits of God's kingdom. It is a guidance that leads to right relationship—a mutuality of relationship between God and all God's people. It can't be copied from the back of the book; it has to be lived! It is a journey of discovery, not a system of salvation.

Jeremiah gives us two further clues about the nature of this mysterious law in our hearts:

- It reflects the dynamic of God—always to bring good out of bad, better out of good, and best out of better. The dynamic of evil works the other way around, always diminishing our good to mediocre, and our poor to worst. Observing how these contradictory movements are working in us at any particular moment is an important tool for cooperating with God's law.
- It is for all God's people, not just for those who understand the rules of discernment. It flows from God's own

presence deep within our hearts, and that presence is often more obvious in those who are not overburdened with their own achievements.

"I will put my law within them, and I will write it on their hearts."

There is a beautiful story of how, one day, God was talking with the angels about where God might hide God's self in creation so that humankind might not find their Creator too easily but might grow through their searching.

The first angel suggested the depths of the earth as a hiding place. "No," said God. "They will soon learn to dig mines, and they will find me too soon."

"What about hiding on their moon?" the second angel suggested. "No," said God. "It won't be long before they reach the moon with their technology. They will find me too soon."

It was the third angel who hit on the Great Idea. "Why don't you hide yourself in their own hearts?" she suggested. "They'll never think to look there." So God did just that, and this is why it takes us so long to find God, step-by-step as we do our living. And that search, in turn, is what makes us grow.

You might like to ask God today to draw you a little closer to the secret depths of your own heart, where God has hidden God's self for you to discover.

Lord, give me the courage to go beyond my ready-made answers and to know you, rather than merely knowing about you. Amen.

Choices

Read Deuteronomy 30:11-19.

T oday we discover a little more about this mysterious "law" that God has written in our own hearts. Do we have to scour the heavens to find it? Do we have to sail beyond the most distant horizons? Do we have to spend our waking moments buried in library books? Do we have to be Martin Luthers or Mother Teresas? Do we have to be ordained or vowed to the monastic life? Do we even have to be tithing members of a church?

Apparently not. The search for this "law," we learn, happens within us, in the context of our everyday living and in the choices we make as we go about our daily life. "The word," God tells us, "is very near to you. You will find it reflected in your own words and actions, choices and relationships. The secret is to learn to live by it."

This is good news and bad news. The good news is that all persons, regardless of intelligence or ability, can search within themselves to discover the guiding of God. The bad news is that this leaves us no excuse for not following it and putting it into practice.

But God doesn't leave us stumbling around in the dark. The Holy One goes on to give us these ground rules for living in alignment with God.

- The nature of God is always to lead in the direction of greater fullness of life. This is God's desire for us. We begin to discover our true "alignment" when this starts to shape our own desiring too.

- However, there are many counterattractions that claim to be giving us a fuller life but are actually distracting us from the quest of our hearts for God. Some of these imposters are obvious, as they crowd into our living rooms each night via TV commercials. Others are much more subtle in their approach.

An important aspect of our journeying is to learn to recognize what form these counterattractions take for each of us personally at any given time or in any given situation, and to seek God's help in dealing with them. We deal with them most effectively by keeping our main focus at all times on what is most important to us—our quest to live true to God's stirrings within us. The strength of this desire is, ultimately, stronger than all the lesser wants and wishes that might pull us off course.

God's great desire is that we should choose life, and choosing life, we learn, is not a one-time decision, but a moment-by-moment affair, reflected (or denied) in everything we do. Every choice we make, every reaction and response to life's events, has the potential to draw us toward a fuller life or to diminish us into something less than the best.

"Choose life."

What might it mean in practice to choose life? Perhaps we need only look again at the way God works. God's way is, as we have seen, always to bring the good out of the less-than-good. So we choose life whenever our own living reflects this dynamic too. This may be in major issues, such as working to resolve a matter of conflict in the family or at work, or it may be as simple as offering a word of encouragement or comfort to someone when we could have chosen to pass by in silence.

And how will we know when we are choosing life? How can we tell whether we are "living true" or not? In the language of our own lives, the words in today's passage might translate into something like this:

- We will feel in tune with ourselves (deep down) when we are following the call to life in small ways or in large.
- We will feel at odds with ourselves (deep down) when we let ourselves be sidetracked by things that are not leading to the fullness of life.

We need to be aware, however, that our surface feelings, in any given situation, may not be so clear. They may deceive us, just as a tree may be swayed violently in its topmost branches though its root is firmly grounded in the earth.

Perhaps we might carry one crucial question around with us as we move through the events of our living: "What does the best in me choose to do?"

Lord, in all I do, the big things and the trivial, help me to stand still for just a moment to ask, "What does the best in me choose to do?" Amen.

Signposts

Read John 1:19-37.

I magine yourself walking along a busy street in your town on a sunny morning. People all around you are going about their business—perhaps hurrying to work, chauffeuring children to school, or opening up shops. But in the midst of it all, one person is standing in the middle of the sidewalk, gazing up to the sky.

Give the scene another five minutes, and no prizes for guessing how the busy street looks now! Some people are still getting on with their daily routine, but meanwhile a large crowd has gathered around the stranger on the sidewalk who is gazing at the sky. Nothing has been spoken. But they all want to know what is so powerfully engaging the attention of this person.

It wouldn't matter now if the person who started it all were simply to walk away. The crowd is no longer interested in that person as such, but in whatever was attracting that person's gaze.

Of course, it would be possible to instigate a scene like this just for the fun of it, staring at nothing at all, then walking away, leaving a fascinated crowd behind you, likewise staring at they-know-not-what. But John the Baptist isn't making a joke. His focus is firmly on the One who is going to have a profound effect on the world and its story from this moment on.

Yet what he actually does, at this moment at least, is not a million miles from the action of our person on the main street. He simply directs the attention of the crowds to something— Someone—beyond themselves. This gives me a big clue about where I might discover God's guidance: *I find God's guidance in those who point beyond themselves*.

When I look back over the years, I can name several people who have been John the Baptist for me. Without exception they have been people whose faces have been turned to God, and whose hearts have been focused on God to such an extent that others were bound to notice and be attracted in the same direction. Usually, I suspect, they never realized the power of their witness. They have been people who were so free of any need for personal status and recognition that they could walk away when their task was done, entrusting the rest to God. And they haven't always been in the places where you might expect such people to be.

By contrast, I have also encountered people, and institutions, who appeared to be doing the opposite—pointing always to themselves rather than to the One who is beyond them. John shows us very graphically how to deal with this tendency toward a "messiah complex" in ourselves and in others. His answer is a simple, honest, straightforward "No." "No, I'm not the One you are looking for. I am only pointing in his direction. I'm not your destination. I'm just one of the signposts along your way." There is a danger in listening to those who claim to have "the answers" in their own right. There is an even greater danger in becoming such a person ourselves.

And when the awaited one actually appears, John readily lets his own disciples move on. He even encourages them to do so. "Look, that's the man you are looking for. Follow him." The Lord is bigger than all our lesser allegiances—even our allegiance to a particular faith tradition.

"Look, here is the lamb of God!"

During this first week of our Advent journey, we have explored just a few of the ways in which God guides us. But we who are guided by God are also called, as John was called, to "prepare the way of the Lord"—to journey on in such a way that we (perhaps unconsciously) provide pointers to those who follow after. We are challenged to live constantly with our inner eyes fixed on God. We are challenged always to point beyond ourselves.

Where have you discovered pointers to God in your personal story? Which way is the finger of your own life pointing?

Lord, please make my own life into a pointer toward you—but please don't let me realize you are doing it, in case I am tempted to turn the signpost back toward myself. Amen.

———∞∞∞———

Glimpses
of Trust

TRUST IS A GIFT that we are born with but very quickly lose as we grow up. Waiting, in the spirit of Advent, asks a special kind of trust that will cooperate with the coming of God into God's world, without knowing the outcome of our waiting or how long that waiting will last.

During the next few days we explore what it is that helps us to trust. What makes trusting possible in an untrustworthy world? We begin by joining Mary of Nazareth as she is asked to entrust her whole being to the unknown of God's incarnation, and we end with Joseph as he too crosses the trust threshold, guided by a dream. As we move through the days, we explore how trust can grow through:

- Listening to our own personal experience of the touch of God upon our lives (December 8)
- Going deep into the "taproot" of our lives, to draw on the resources that flow from God, who is at home in the core of our being (December 9)
- Surrender to the certainty that the Creator knows the ways of life better than the creature does (December 10)
- The discovery that life's simplest aspects are more trustworthy than its many complications (December 11)
- Learning to discern the difference between the kind of power that seeks to control us and may need to be resisted, and the kind of power that transforms us and commands our loving obedience (December 12)
- The call to be adventurers, investing all we have in the onward journey with the Lord (December 13)
- The potential of our intuitive depths to expose the deeper dreaming below our life's nightmares (December 14)

Experience

Read Luke 1:26–38.

I sometimes ask myself what actually keeps me believing in the
Good News. Is it because someone else says it is true? That
might have worked when I was a child, but it certainly wouldn't
have been enough to keep me with it through the challenges of
adult life. Is it because if I don't keep believing, I may miss out
on "eternal life"? No again. Because that would be a faith based
on fear, and fear, though it can force us into doing things we don't
want or intend to do, can never move our hearts or ignite our
vision. When I really get to the heart of what keeps me believing, I discover it is actually something that on the surface appears
to be intangible and rather fragile—it is my own personal experience of the times and the ways in which God has touched my
life. Sometimes this touch of God has brought healing or comfort when I thought I was at the end of my rope. Sometimes it
has given me the strength to stay in a difficult place or the courage
to make necessary changes. Sometimes it has momentarily set
my soul alight in a flash of joy that has given me energy to keep
moving on, trusting that this experience was coming from a
bedrock reality far deeper than my own small conscious world.

Mary's encounter with the angel Gabriel is perhaps one such
moment of experience, written large! What made her able to say
"Yes!" to the angel's request? Mary had certainly been brought
up in faithful obedience to the Jewish law, but I find it hard to
believe that this alone gave her the trust to hand over her future;

37

her reputation; her body, mind, and soul to God as she did. And though the coming of the angel must have summoned up her fears, these fears seem to have been more like an overwhelming sense of awe at a presence that was larger than life, rather than the fear of something that was bringing harm. Fear alone might have elicited a terrified consent from her, but it would never have kept her faithful through all that was to come.

What seems to have set Mary's soul on fire that morning was surely her own personal, direct experience of the presence of God, granted to her through the vision of the angel. This was so overwhelming, so joy-filled, such an eternal moment, that she would never again doubt the power and the ever-presence of the God from whom it came. "Yes!" was the only possible response to such an experience.

I also find it strangely consoling to learn that Mary immediately questioned her own experience. Most of us can identify with her questioning. One moment we can feel God's touch upon our life; the next moment we find ourselves saying, "This can't be true, because it doesn't fit within my familiar parameters!" The angel counters this questioning not with simple black-and-white answers, but with an assurance that God's ways are infinitely larger than our minds and hearts can ever encompass. Our own rules and patterns can never contain God's transforming power. All we can do—all we are asked to do—is to allow that transforming power to be "earthed" in our own living. "Nothing is impossible to God!" All our mind-sets are just matchbox-size when it comes to holding the immensity and the potential of God.

Yet this power is not threatening. The angel's first word to Mary is "Rejoice!" rapidly followed by the assurance that there is nothing to fear. In the light of all that is to come, this might sound like unwarranted optimism. Do we really have nothing to fear if we say our own "Yes!" to God? Perhaps, again, it is a question of the size of our mind-set. To our "matchbox" thinking, there may well be challenges along the way ahead that will give rise to fear. But the angel's promise is that the overwhelming love of God will always be infinitely stronger than the pull of all our fears. We are not promised an easy "happy ever after." What we are promised is that the joy we experience when God touches our hearts is the real thing, and nothing else that can happen to us, however difficult or frightening, will ever have more power than that touch. The way of God always leads to new life.

"Let it be with me according to your word."

In the days ahead, we reflect on what it means to wait for God's coming with trust in our hearts. Mary reveals that the basis for this trust is to be found in our own experience. Take a little time to remember those moments in your own life when God seemed especially close. How did you feel then? What was your response? What difference did your experience make to your ongoing journey through life?

Lord, please keep my own heart's "Yes!" alive through all the questions that may follow. Bring to birth in my life what you conceived in me when your life touched mine. Be with me in all the labor pains that may come, until together we rejoice over the "you" you have birthed in me. Amen.

Depth

Read Jeremiah 17:5-8.

It doesn't take a degree in biology to understand that a plant has the best chance of staying alive if its roots can reach deep sources of water and nourishment. The plant that relies only on its flowers and leaves to keep it going is unlikely to survive the hard times. When the going gets tough, living things return to their deeper sources for the means to survive, whether the threat is from the droughts of summer or the frosts of winter. They return to a root that is deeper than anything we can see at ground level. Perhaps we can learn from them something of what we ourselves need, if our trust in God's companionship and action in our lives is to survive the obstacles it will undoubtedly encounter.

When I look out the window and see the spreading oak tree outside, its branches help me to return to this "deeper root." Sometimes, in prayer and in my daily living, I find myself astride the horns of a dilemma: *If I do this, I can't do that* or *If this is the right course, the other course must be wrong.* The oak tree outside the window has many forked branches. If I were a squirrel, I could go so far along such a branch, but when I arrived at the fork, I would have to choose which direction to follow. Sometimes my choice is guided by the presence of something I desire that is to be found along one of the "branches" and not, apparently, along the other. As a squirrel, for example, I might choose the branch that seems to lead to more acorns. Sometimes the choice seems entirely random, guided only by my intuition or the whim of the moment.

Often these everyday choices are unimportant. But sometimes major issues are involved, such as "Which church community do I choose to join?" And the more that is at stake, the more tempting it is to assume that one "branch" is "right" and all other options are "wrong." That makes it much easier for me to choose and to stay with my choice in the future. I can't be on two branches at once, so the more firmly I can justify my choice, the better.

Unfortunately, these assumptions about the "right" and the "wrong" way are usually ill-founded. Life is rarely black-and-white. Often the best we can do is to choose the branch that is more life-giving for us right now, and yet to hold that choice in the light of a deeper understanding that other branches may offer the more life-giving choice for other people or in different situations. That is where the forked branches in the oak tree become my wise teachers. They show me how all the branches can be traced back to a deeper root. There is a point, further down the tree, where they join as one. Their separateness is merely a manifestation of a deeper oneness in the base of the branch, in the trunk, and in the taproot.

The taproot is what keeps the tree alive. And the same is true for our soul survival. At the branch level of our existence, anything can happen. There are no guarantees, no insurance policies. Storms might rip through our branches, or lightning might set them on fire. The heat of the sun might split them, or blight might kill them. Yet the "tree" of our being is rooted in God, and that taproot lies too deep to be subject to the volatile world above ground. Even more than this, our taproot is something that is common to us all. The deeper we go in our journeying with God, the closer we come together, at home in the ground of our being, far deeper than the fences that divide us. At that depth we share intimately in one another's struggles, and we are nourished by one another's trust.

At these depths, there is often darkness. We do not, and cannot, know how our growing is working itself out, or how long it will take before we come into the fullness of our being. But the taproot is the source of all the nourishment we need to keep us going through the dark unknowing. We can connect to this taproot in the silence of prayer, asking God simply to hold us in the darkness, to feed us in ways we cannot understand or explain.

". . . like a tree planted by water, sending out its roots by the stream"

During the Second World War, many Londoners survived the blitz by going deep into the underground, where bombs could not penetrate. Life can still feel like a bombing raid, even in peacetime. Job security can disappear overnight, and the pension funds that our retirement depends on can be wiped out at the click of a mouse on a finance company's computer screen. Disease can strike us down. Friends can betray us and lovers abandon us. Perhaps you know some of these "bombs" in your own life. Where do you seek shelter in these circumstances? When the sirens of misfortune wail through your life, do you know the way to the underground?

In wartime, everyone knew the way to the nearest air-raid shelter. Each person's survival depended on that knowledge. In the same way, the survival of your deepest being depends on your knowing how to draw life-strength from your deepest roots.

Where are those roots for you? What sustains you when everything else lets you down? If the branches of your life—those projects or relationships that you value—are struck by lightning, where is your taproot? What connects you to the ground of your being?

How familiar are you with the access routes to that deeper root? One way to become familiar with the way down to your taproot is to keep using it, in prayer, until eventually it will be second nature to you, and you will be able to find it in the darkest night.

Lord, I live "above ground" for most of my waking moments. Teach me the way to my taproot in you. Clear the deepest channels of my being so that your love and grace can flow freely to the exposed edges of my living. Amen.

Surrender

Read Isaiah 64:8 and Jeremiah 18:1-6.

A friend of mine, who is blind, recently made a visit to a local pottery manufacturer, where visitors were invited to try their hand at the potter's wheel and experience for themselves how it would feel to mold and shape a lump of clay. To make this possible for my friend, the potter who was demonstrating his craft offered to work with him. And so my friend described to me afterward the experience of feeling the wet clay beneath his hands, but also the gentle strength of the potter's hands guiding his own, as they shaped the clay together.

This story helps me relate in a new way to the image of God as the Potter. It also leads me to reflect on whose hands are forming my life. Are they God's hands and the hands of those who help shape me in and through God's love? Or are they the hands of other people, waiting in the wings to shape me into a mold that suits their own purposes? Or are there perhaps no guiding hands at all, because I am sometimes so determined to do it all my way?

I came to the conclusion that for much of my life I have allowed—and continue to allow—other factors to shape me in ways that may not be God's ways. Sometimes these are other people who may or may not mean well and could be misguided or even manipulative in their clumsy attempts to mold the clay of my life. Sometimes these alien factors may be circumstances that I meet, which I too often allow to shape my course in ways that, on deeper reflection, I might not have chosen.

Small wonder, then, that my "pot" so often turns pear-shaped! And God, as Jeremiah reminds us, has to begin again, flattening out the mess and reshaping it over and over, with endless patience. Would that I had that kind of patience too! The waiting time seems to last forever, punctuated by one failed pot after another and a long process of reshaping and re-forming.

How can I learn to trust this process more deeply? When my life is, so to speak, on the potter's wheel, trust is often a long way from my heart. The wheel of circumstances seems to spin so wildly. The pressure of the potter's hands—so firm and gentle when God is the Potter—can sometimes take me almost to the breaking point when those hands are not God's. I feel only the pressure and the dizziness. How can I trust that the Potter knows what the Potter is doing?

One thing that helps me discern when my life is being shaped by the eternal Potter is the purpose of the pot as it starts to take shape. A pot is made to hold something and to offer that something to others—food or drink, perhaps, or flowers. When God's hand is guiding the circumstances of my life, the result will be something for others, however small. God the Potter is God the Giver. To trust the process that leads to this result, I am asked to surrender my own limited thoughts and views of what should happen to the larger vision of the Creator-Potter, who knows what the divine hand is making and why.

Would that we could always let God do the shaping, trusting in God's vision when we ourselves have as yet no clue to what is becoming of us. We fail, of course. Over and over we surrender our freedom to the wrong hands, or we claim the right to shape ourselves, and God begins again. But today's readings give us hope that getting things wrong is never the final word. Reshaping is always a possibility. God doesn't power down the wheel at clocking-out time and go home in despair. The very fact that my failures and breakdowns happen is another sign that God is the master Potter, however many other would-be potters, including myself, interfere with the process.

Yesterday we found a source of trustfulness by going to a deeper root of our being. Today we discover trust in the simple fact that the potter knows better than the clay. Ultimately, the clay has no choice but to surrender to the potter's hands. Certainly, we can resist the potter's touch, just as a child can resist the guidance of a loving parent. But our resistance can, at worst, only prolong the process of our becoming. It has no power to override the potter's vision for his new creation.

"Like the clay in the potter's hand, so are you in my hand."

Try shaping a piece of clay in your hands, or if this isn't possible, try to imagine yourself doing so. That shaping is helped greatly by the warmth of your hands and by their moisture. Where does the warmth come from in the shaping of your life? Where is the moisture? Perhaps your tears are a necessary ingredient.

The process through which God shapes God's dream in our lives is always done by hand. It is a process of intimate contact. Intimacy requires trust, as it invites us to surrender to the touch of God's love, so deeply personal, shaping us uniquely. No mass production on God's workbench; no two pots alike in God's kingdom; and, in the end, no waste!

Lord, I ask for the grace to love you enough to trust you, and to trust you enough to let you shape me into someone who will offer your love back to your creation. Amen.

Simplicity

Read Luke 12:22-32.

Two surprises dropped into my life recently, one good and one not so good. First the bad news. This came in the form of a statement from a trust fund we have that is supposed to pay for our daughter's years in medical school. The statement informed me that the fund isn't doing well at all.

With a wry smile I remembered the fine print, which says investments like these can go down as well as up. I thought about all those people in the city, sitting at their PCs, clicking their way through rows and rows of figures. I thought about all the fund managers in their smart suits, weighing the relative prospects of this company or the other, and moving money around the world in some endless poker game, stressing themselves into heart attacks and strokes. I thought of all the board meetings and shareholders' gatherings, debating what to do through every new crisis.

The end result of all my pondering came to zero. There is absolutely nothing I can do to make the fund more fruitful. Nor does it appear to be possible for all those busy executives to "add a single hour" to its existence! So I may as well get on with my life and stop worrying.

But the good news went a long way to make up for this setback. At the end of our garden is a field. The farmer who works it has had a bad year. The weather has been unkind to him. The crop he sowed in spring failed and had to be plowed under again. Now the field is green with a grass crop, just as the autumn is settling in.

The surprise came in the shape of a magnificent sunflower, standing proud, right in the middle of this field—all alone, in solitary splendor! For some time we have watched this little "alien" growing there, a spot of darker green among the grass. Eventually it became obvious that it was going to be something special, and this week it came into its glory. Its dinner-plate flower is fully open now, exuberantly golden, its head raised proudly to the skies, lord of all it surveys.

Back in the wet, dark days of last autumn, a sunflower seed must have dropped into the soggy furrows of that field. No one knew about the event. The farmer had no idea it was there, nor did we—though I suspect God may have had an inkling of what was happening!

Through the wind and rain of winter it germinated down there in the field. No one helped it along. No one brought any fertilizer or put it in a greenhouse. It just got on with the job of becoming what it was always meant to be—unheard, unseen, unregarded—until when the time was right it thrust its whole being through the clay soil and presented itself to creation.

While the sunflower was in bloom, we had a group of people in our home for a quiet day. At the end of the day they were sharing their reflections on what the day's quiet prayer had meant for them, and each of them had something to say about that sunflower. "A messenger from God," one person described it. "Just to remind us that God is making us into the people God dreams us to be, without any of our own doing."

"A sign for me," said another, "that the seed that no one planted and no one tended can become the most beautiful growth in the whole field."

"A promise," suggested a third, "that if God can delight and surprise us with a solitary sunflower in a field, how much more God will do in our lives if we will only let God do so."

"I tell you, do not worry about your life."

Look back over how your week has been so far. What has bogged you down and sent you into "worry mode"? Have there been any "sunflowers" around to remind you that trusting God to grow you into who you really are is almost too simple to be true?

Lord of the stock markets and the sunflower seeds, give me the grace to trust the silent growth of your seed in my heart and to let that trust grow stronger and taller than all my worries. Amen.

Obedience

Read John 2:1-11.

In my youth, like many children, I guess, I frequently demanded to know why I was being asked to do something, or more often, to refrain from doing something—to which the parental reply would come back, "Because I say so!" At the time, I promised myself that I would never give such unsatisfactory answers to my own children, but needless to say, I failed in that undertaking!

Here we find Jesus himself, or rather his mother on his behalf, saying very much the same kind of thing. "Don't ask questions. Just do it! Do as he tells you!" It sounds like a demand for blind obedience, which raises big questions in the minds of generations who have witnessed the horrors of the Holocaust and the extremes into which blind obedience can lead. And yet here, at Cana, this demand for obedience was the necessary condition for Jesus' first miracle, the first manifestation of his power to transform.

When is it appropriate to obey, and when is it right to resist? When should we remain within legitimate boundaries, and when is it our duty to break out of oppressive limitations? I find it fascinating to discover Jesus himself grappling with these thoughts, when his mother first points out to him that the wine has run out. At first he seems to want to stay within the boundaries. "Why are you telling me this? Don't challenge me to take action here. It's not the right time." But Mary's intuition prevails, that this is indeed the right time and that God's transforming power is beginning to flow through her son. She acts on her intuition and issues the instruction to "do whatever he tells you." This seems to push Jesus over the boundary, releasing the latent power of God within him. He becomes obedient to the demands of this new power, and the servants, in turn, proceed to do as they have been told with unquestioning obedience. The obedience both of Jesus to his Father and of the servants to Jesus is based on trust. They can only imagine where this act of obedience will lead.

The question of power and authority is high on the world's agenda today, and it is the source of much heart-searching within the church too. *Power* is a loaded word. Perhaps it is so loaded because, for the most part, we experience the exercise of power in our world as an oppressive force, enslaving people, engendering fear, and centered on the "kingdom" of the power wielder rather than on the reign of God. We see it, justifiably, as the power to control. We know that such power cannot be trusted, and we instinctively want to resist.

At Cana, however, a very different kind of power is being released—the power to transform. Jesus' ability to change the water into wine is a sign—the first sign—of God's unimaginable power to transform our broken creation into an eternity of love and of life. Jesus is far from wanting to control the situation, as his hesitation reveals. But he is willing to obey the promptings of the Father to open up a channel of transformation. When transformation is the source and the intention of power, obedience is the appropriate response—even blind obedience—because we are being touched here by things we cannot begin to understand, yet know we can trust and are called to cooperate with.

Through the miracle at Cana, Jesus revealed his glory, and the disciples believed in him. The power that transforms inspires our trust. This kind of power flows from authentic authority. The authority of Jesus is rooted in the Father, the Author of all being. This is the only kind of authority we are asked to trust, but we are asked to trust it completely and be obedient to its action in our lives and in our hearts.

"Do whatever he tells you."

Who, or what, exerts power in your life? In what ways is obedience expected of you, and what is the agenda behind this expectation? Without making any judgments, either of yourself or of others, just notice:

- What channels of power and authority in your life tend to control and enslave you in some way, engendering fear and serving the agenda of someone else's "kingdom"? How do you feel about your reaction to these power centers?

- Where do you see evidence of transforming power in your life? (Perhaps in significant relationships or the demands of a life-giving cause or project.) In what ways do you feel you are being asked to cooperate with this kind of power, maybe without any explanations in advance as to how it will all work out?

Lord, open our eyes to recognize and resist the powers that seek to control us, but also to trust and cooperate with your power that longs to transform us. Amen.

Adventure

Read John 1:35–39.

Every tiny step in the process of evolution is a step beyond the comfort zone—and every such step is a step taken in trust. Since the first primitive sea creatures set tentative foot on the hazardous terrain of dry land, all creation has been moving and growing in this global adventure of life. Our spiritual growth, surely, is no exception to this universal pattern.

I grew up before aliens, dinosaurs, and disaster movies took over the TV screens, in the days when major epics centered on the journeys of pioneers across America in wagon trains. I remember watching, fascinated, as families would sell everything they owned in order to buy the wagon and the oxen and a few pots and pans for the trek west, across completely uncharted land. Then, with only the wisdom and courage of a scout to help them find the way and protect themselves against whatever dangers they might encounter, they would set out on journeys of thousands of miles to follow their dream.

"What vision might be worth a venture like that?" I ask myself. For those early pioneers, the vision that impelled them onward was perhaps about freedom, a new start in a new world, and riches and well-being that were unimaginable in the slums of Europe or downtown New York. It was also an expression of the insatiable quest in humankind to know what lies beyond our present experience. Perhaps this quest is right at the heart of everything we call adventure.

An adventure is about to happen on the morning described in today's reading. Its beginnings are very modest. The curious gaze of two young men follows the steps of a traveling rabbi. The man who has been their leader until now makes no attempt to hold them back. Instead, he urges them to follow the stranger. They have no rational way of knowing that this man Jesus will lead them to their deepest desiring. We, who follow after, know that the quest into which Jesus leads us is also about freedom, a new start in a world God is renewing, and a spiritual wealth and well-being beyond anything we could ever provide for ourselves. He invites us, just as he invited them, into the great adventure of "come and see." For us the terrain of this journey is by no means as unknown as it was for John's disciples, yet it remains God's mystery. For each of us, the adventure will take a different route, but it will always call us beyond our comfort zone.

We might notice three steps to adventure in this story:

1. We need the courage to take just that first step in pursuit of our dream.
2. We need to reflect on what is really at the heart of our dream. What do we want?
3. We need to follow, with complete trust, wherever the dream may lead.

The disciples take the first step to discover the identity of this man who so holds their attention. When they follow him, he challenges them with the question "What do you want?" and invites them to make a journey of trust, without telling them where it will lead. "Come and see," he says.

One important way in which we exercise trust is by stepping out in courage. To take that first step in following our dream is an act of trust. Trust is not necessarily a state of passivity, but often one of expectant readiness. To trust in the One who calls us to "come and see" is to be ready, if necessary, to let go of everything we thought was so important, in order to have the resources to "buy our wagon" and move on.

A wise adventurer travels light. The early American pioneers who had loaded up their wagons with all kinds of extras were the ones who got stuck on the steep inclines and had to jettison the things they hadn't been able to leave behind them. When they follow Jesus, John's disciples are leaving behind the people, places, and situations that have until then provided them with identity and security. Our own journey of trust may ask no less of us. The more baggage we are carrying with us, in terms of emotional or material dependencies, the more likely we are to become stuck at the first major hurdle. Can we trust the One who calls us enough to let everything else in our lives slip into second place behind our deepest desire to be discoverers and cocreators of God's reign on earth?

"Come and see."

What form has the adventure of faith taken for you, so far, in your life? Look back, if you can, to the very first steps, and remember the trust in which you set out. What vision inspired you? Can you see any ways in which your trust has strengthened with each subsequent step along the way?

The particular path you are walking has never been walked before. You are pioneering it, with Jesus as your "scout." You are learning to trust him. Stop to reflect today on just how much he trusts you to pioneer your personal route through the tangle of creation, so that God's grace may flow freely through that unique combination of circumstances.

Lord, I don't know where we are going, but I trust your invitation to "come and see." Give me the courage to invest everything I have and everything I am in the great adventure of life in you. Amen.

Dreaming

Read Matthew 1:18–25.

How close the connections, it sometimes seems, between our dreams and our nightmares! Today we are reminded of the nightmare that unfolded in Joseph's life as a result of Mary's pregnancy. It may help you to empathize with his situation if you can recall any major crisis in your own life, and the many conflicting feelings it brought up in you, along with all the agonized heart-searching about what to do and how to respond to the changed circumstances.

It is perhaps all too easy to leave Mary and Joseph safely and cozily in the tableau of a nativity play. Looking into the real heartache and very present dangers that faced them as a direct result of Mary's "Yes" to God is often something we would rather avoid.

Yet the way through this apparent deadlock—this nightmare that must end, at the very least, in a heartbreaking divorce—opens up, paradoxically, in a dream. The story records how Joseph came to a deeper understanding of God's meaning in this confusion when he was fast asleep. When his normal conscious thought processes were in abeyance, Joseph's heart became receptive to new possibilities—possibilities that defied reason, yet rang deeply true. This story holds out more hope for us today than perhaps we even dare to imagine.

We don't need to search too far to discover our own twenty-first-century incarnations of Joseph's nightmare. At a personal level we grapple with our own difficult relationships, conflicts, and moral dilemmas. As a human family, we face sudden and terrible upheavals from both natural and humanly created disasters. Our certainties, hopes, and expectations can be dashed overnight, like sandcastles on the seashore. What can we do when life takes us by the throat in this kind of way and squeezes the very breath out of us? In his own way, Joseph knew the flavor of that personal nightmare. And for him the deeper answer lay concealed within a dream.

To get in touch with the deeper dream, it may be necessary to change gear and focus not on the feelings that were aroused by the tragedy itself, but rather on any new life that ultimately grew from it. There are, I believe, trees in the Australian outback that are regularly destroyed by forest fires. Yet the forests regenerate over and over again. They do so because their seeds burst open only when they are exposed to the kind of high temperatures that occur in a fire. The coming of new growth is built into the tree's nature. The dream of the new life is latent in the ashes of the old.

If we take a look at some of our own tragedies—either personal or global—in this light, we may detect similar new growth. Personal breakdown often releases a new spurt of personal growth, the development of a new depth of wisdom and compassion, or new insights into alternative ways forward. Global disaster can release the very best in humankind—the overwhelming and universal desire to preserve the sanctity of life, to rescue those in danger, to comfort and tend those who are hurt or in grief. The dream of all that is best in us is latent in the wreckage of the worst we can do to one another.

So today's reading might lead us to reflect that one way to deal with the nightmare scenarios in our life can be to go deeper, down to the layers of our being that lie below politics and cultural patterning, there to discover the fragments of God that inhabit our hearts and draw us together in our common humanity when circumstances seem to be hurling us apart.

We must thank God that Joseph does not act out of the nightmare going on at the surface of his life, but out of the dream that inhabits the core of his being. If he had stayed with the surface nightmare, he might well have wanted to lash out in anger against the unseen, unknown father of his fiancée's child. A ludicrous idea? Yet one we all too easily embody in our own "surface" thinking and reacting—and history teaches us the results. The dream reveals another way.

And Joseph, in his zero hour, when his hopes of marriage, his faith, and his relationship with the girl he loves have crumbled into dust, teaches us how to make that other way a reality in our own lives. He trusts the dream, and he acts upon it.

"An angel of the Lord appeared to him in a dream."

Take time this week to look at a newspaper. You will read about some aspect of "the nightmare" for sure, but notice too the scattered evidence of the deeper dream—the God-with-us, the best that is at the core of our being and is always there, like a silent angel, for those who have eyes to see. Which will you trust? Which will you act upon?

Lord, below the world's nightmares lies your indestructible dream. We catch glimpses of it in moments of compassion, heroism, resilience, and all expressions of authentic human loving. Give us grace to trust the dream, especially when it seems to be buried in the ash and debris of our lives. Amen.

————⦾————

Glimpses
of Wisdom

NOT ALL GUIDANCE comes from outside ourselves. A pool of deep wisdom also lies in the core of our being, and we can learn to discern what within ourselves can be trusted and what cannot. During the next few days we focus on the slow growth of that wisdom and that discernment, and how we might cooperate in its growth.

We begin by joining Mary as she makes her response to God's action in her life in the words of the Magnificat—an expression that surrenders itself to the greater reality within and beyond itself, and lets that wisdom spill out to touch all creation.

- Our search for the wisdom that is God's own wisdom then leads us to discover how much wider and deeper is God's perspective, relative to our own (December 15).
- We join Solomon in his discerning of what makes for true wisdom (December 16).
- We look at which seeds in our life are growing into wholesome harvest, and which are not (December 17).
- We allow God to grow us by moving us gently beyond our comfort zones (December 18).
- We explore what it means to wait in readiness for God's advent into our lives (December 19).
- We reflect on how personal suffering can draw us into deeper levels of wisdom and understanding (December 20).
- Finally, we share in the meeting between Mary and Elizabeth, and learn from them the power of recognizing in one another the Christ who is coming to birth in each of us (December 21).

Perspective

Read Luke 1:46-55.

With these words of prayer and praise, Mary begins her personal "waiting time," and we might allow them to lead us into what it means for us personally to be waiting expectantly, as she is, for the coming of God into our lives and our world.

The child she is carrying has already overturned her world, her hopes of a quiet life, even her religious expectations. It's one thing to believe in the coming of the Messiah who will become the liberator of his people Israel; it's quite another matter to be invited to bring that Messiah to birth oneself! All that is going to happen in the thirty or so years that lie ahead will challenge Mary's expectations over and over again. Events will move her, at breakneck speed, beyond the "received wisdom" that has come to her from the teachings of the Jewish faith and her family upbringing to a radically new kind of wisdom that will emerge from the depths of her own heart, under the guidance of the Spirit of the child she carries.

This process of gaining a very different perspective on God's wisdom begins the moment Jesus is conceived in her. From this moment, Mary's understanding of God's ways widens and deepens. It is a perspective that goes right back to her spiritual roots, and the roots of her people, but also extends far forward to a kingdom that is yet to come.

In a few days we will spend some time with Hannah, who prayed for a child, whose prayer was granted, and who then gave that child, Samuel, over to the Lord's service. Hannah, too, when she knew that she was at last pregnant with Samuel, expressed her joy in a prayer very similar to Mary's Magnificat (see 1 Sam. 2:1–10). Luke makes sure we make this connection in our minds, by stressing the similarities between both women's prayers. Mary is speaking the language of her forebears in faith in her thanksgiving to God. Implicitly, she too is acknowledging that her child is also given over to the Lord, whatever that may come to mean for her as the years unfold.

So there is a looking back and a looking forward. When a child is born, this extended perspective is always evident. People look for family traits and resemblances in the new life, and they also express hopes for its future. Often threads of family connectedness are rewoven at such a time, but for the parents at least, there is a radical change to their future expectations. Anyone whose life has ever been touched by the presence of a new baby knows what power such a tiny being has to overturn and unsettle us. Wisdom begins to dawn that human life is both utterly fragile and vulnerable, and utterly awesome in its power to shape and transform creation. We stand before the mystery that everything we are, as individuals, began long before human memory, when God's love first spilled over into creation, and extends far beyond our own life span, affecting for good or ill everything and everyone following after us. We also realize that this private event for a particular family is always a public event as well, with the potential to shape the course of human evolution in some unique way. Every birth is both a moment in history and a manifestation of mystery. This is wisdom that God grants to every human heart that has ever beheld the wonder of new life.

The novelist Victor Hugo once commented that "more powerful than all the armies in the world is an idea whose time is come." You may recognize in your own life those projects that were unstoppable because "the time was right," while ideas that you may have desperately strained to bring to fruition came to nothing if their time had not yet come. As we pause alongside Mary at the moment of Jesus' conception, we are witnessing the moment when God's idea has come to its time. Life itself is God's idea, and this Christ child is given to us to bring life in all its fullness. That fullness will be a kingdom where gentleness prevails over force, humility over arrogance, simplicity over extravagance. The time has come. Nothing on earth can stop the fulfilling of God's idea, now that Mary has said her "Yes." The divine revolution is underway!

"The Mighty One has done great things for me."

What begins with Mary's "Yes" is to be continued in every human life, until Alpha evolves into Omega and all creation is restored to its original wholeness. Each of us is invited in a unique way to engage our life's energy in the great venture of making God's idea a reality in our world. Take a moment to reflect on the times in your life when you have become aware of the radical wisdom of God touching your life in some particular way—perhaps a moment of insight, or the certainty that a particular choice should be made. What difference have such times made to you? Write your personal "Magnificat," if you feel drawn to do so.

Lord, take all that we have received from the past, and grow and transform it into all that we shall become, in the fullness of the kingdom. Amen.

Discernment

Read 1 Kings 3:4-15.

Yesterday, Mary's Magnificat gave us a starting point for our exploration of what it means to wait expectantly for God's wisdom by showing us that whatever this wisdom is about, it is rooted in our own humility. To the extent that we can begin to recognize the impossibility of bringing anything to birth on our own, we become open to God's action in our living. To the extent that we remain determined to "do our own thing" in our own way, we block that action.

Today Solomon is dreaming! Deep in his psyche lies the overwhelming question of how he can possibly cope with the demands coming down on him. He has become king in succession to his illustrious father, David, but, as he confesses, he has really no idea what to do next. He is young, inexperienced in leadership, and feels very much the shadow of his father hanging over every move he makes. I wonder how we would react to a newly elected prime minister who had the honesty to confess his or her feelings of inadequacy with such disarming candor. I hope we would welcome it as a sign that at last our national and international relations might have a chance of beginning from a place of integrity and humility.

Dare we risk being so vulnerable before God, let alone in the hearing of those we want to admire us? Solomon's dream urges him to take this risk. In the dream, God invites him to choose the gift he most wants, to help him master the challenges that lie ahead.

Well, life for a king would be easier, certainly, if his enemies were all eliminated. The power to scare away all opposition is a very tempting gift. We choose it every time we invest our resources in weapons of defense, at the expense of the tools of growth and well-being. We choose it every time we silence or diminish an ethnic minority in our society or condone violence against them, or put down a friend or colleague.

Then again, for the power wielder who doesn't want blood on his hands, a welcome gift would be the financial resources to buy off anyone who poses a threat. With these resources, commercial exploitation can replace weapons of war, leaving less visible, but no less real, carnage in its wake. At a personal level, a gift like this enables us to purchase "friendship," to appease potential hostility, and to ensure that we live among like-minded people.

And then, of course, to enjoy the security and comfort we have purchased with our gifts of power and wealth, we need the extra bonus of a long life in which to enjoy it.

Solomon says, "No." The temptations are obvious, but Solomon's dream points to another way. He chooses the gift of a discerning heart, to judge rightly the better way of dealing with every situation that life may throw at him as a leader and as an individual human being. Such a gift offers absolutely no insurance against the "enemy at the door" and no guarantee of a comfortable lifestyle. What it holds out to us is the possibility of living our own lives, both publicly and privately, in a way that is centered not on our fears or our greed, but on the deep wisdom of God.

The gift is gladly granted. And what God bestows on Solomon, God bestows with equal joy on all persons who honestly want wisdom to be the first priority in their living and the prime yardstick for their choices and decisions. The dream goes further: If we were truly able to make every choice based on this deeper discernment, aligned with the wisdom of God, we would discover that our lesser priorities would also fall into place, and our human need for security and comfort would be satisfied without the need to exploit or threaten one another.

"Ask what I should give you."

Let God put the same question to you that he put to Solomon. What one gift would you ask for as the greatest help in dealing with the choices and events and relationships in your life right now? Don't answer too hastily. Consider carefully all the options, and acknowledge whatever fears and needs they reveal, bringing them to God in the center of honesty and vulnerability at the core of your being.

Lord, when we don't know what we want, please give us the one thing that we really need. Amen.

Seeds

Read Mark 4:26-32.

Wisdom grows slowly! Often we might well feel that God's wisdom in our hearts is not growing at all. Much as we may desire to follow Solomon in asking God for the gift, above all, of a discerning heart and wise judgment in all we do, more often than not we act on different priorities entirely. Even more disturbingly, we frequently find that the roots of the bad things that happen to us lead back to choices we or others made in the past, that were based not on wisdom but on fear or the desire for personal gain. What grows from these flawed seeds may overwhelm us with the ferocity of what it yields when harvest time comes round.

When we listen to the international news, we can discover, almost every night, the evidence of some deadly crop that is growing in the world's fields because in earlier times we have sown bad seed like this. The crimes and even the mistakes and misjudgments of past generations fester on, continuing to haunt our efforts to make our world a place of peace and mutual respect. The abused child can become a child abuser. The violated victim can turn into a violent oppressor of others.

In the musical *Les Miserables*, the boy revolutionary Gavroche puts these warnings into a song that reminds us that if we abuse a dog while it is just a puppy, we should beware of what may happen when the pup becomes a full-grown Rottweiler!

We all know that if we sow the wind we will reap the whirlwind. Tragically, one generation's "wind" becomes the next generation's "whirlwind." And the growth from breeze to hurricane happens so stealthily that we never see it coming.

If such terrible consequences can grow from the bad seeds we sow when we are not living in the light of a higher wisdom, what good fruits, in contrast, might grow from the seeds of love and justice and hope that we sow?

Last night I had a phone call from my oldest friend to tell me that her mother, Alice, had died. We shared our sorrow across an international phone line, and as we were reminiscing, I remembered vividly an incident from our childhood. I was a frequent visitor then at my friend's home, and her parents always made me feel welcome. One afternoon we were all sitting in their house looking out over their back garden, and Alice drew my attention to a riot of exotic growth in the flower bed in the middle of their little back lawn. It looked like something out of the botanical gardens. There were flowers there that none of us had ever seen before. "Where on earth did they all come from?" I asked, mystified. Alice pointed to the bird table at the edge of the flower bed. "Last winter I got some birdseed and put it out there for the birds to help themselves. I guess they must have dropped some, and this is what it grew into!"

We laughed, then, at the amazing harvest that had grown, so slowly and steadily through the winter months, to yield such a crop. And last night, too, on the phone, our tears began to turn into a glimmer of returning joy as we remembered other seeds that Alice had sown, perhaps unknowingly, in our childhood experience. Seeds of compassion and integrity, the love that cherishes and the faith that keeps going. I can easily see the harvest of those seeds now in my friend's life, which is dedicated to God and God's people in ways she is too humble to see for herself.

Today we reap the harvest of Alice's seeding, all those years ago, and we in turn are asked to plow these good seeds back into the earth we will one day leave behind, so that generations still unborn will also rejoice in unexpected blossoms. The process is continuous. The product is beyond our sight. But the choice, to sow good or bad seed in any given situation, is ours to make day by day.

"The seed would sprout and grow, he does not know how."

For most of us, the "flower bed" of our lives will contain a bewildering mixture of weeds and blossoms. Take a while to wander around your own life's flower bed, just noticing what is growing there. If you see things you don't like and would like to uproot, notice what seeds they have grown from, and ask God to do any weeding that is necessary. Rejoice in the blossoms and fruits. What seeds have given life to these good things? Express your thanks in whatever way feels right.

You can be sure of one thing: Good fruit can only come from good seed. Whatever is fruitful and life-giving in your experience comes ultimately from God, the source of life. Whatever is destructive comes from things that are not rooted in God. Let what you find shape tomorrow's choices in some specific way.

Lord, please give us the grace to look carefully, in the light of your wisdom, at the seeds we scatter in the course of our daily living, that they may become a good and wholesome harvest for those who will reap what we sow. Amen.

Growth

Read 1 Samuel 1:20-28; 2:18-21.

The world is shrinking, so we often hear. Journeys that used to take weeks are covered in hours. Distances that used to separate us from friends and loved ones in different countries, or even in different villages, are readily bridged today by air and road, by satellite and e-mail. Our planet has become, as we say, a "global village." Everything has shrunk to a distance within the reach of all of us.

But there is a flip side to this shrinkage. As the world becomes ever "smaller," our own minds and hearts are challenged to expand, to make space for more and more of its concerns. When the globe was vast, and the next village a day's journey away, all we had to deal with were the concerns of those in our immediate neighborhood. By and large, what went on in the rest of the world remained a closed book. Now that the world has become so relatively small, the concerns of everyone have opened up to us. It is no longer possible to close our eyes to the issues that affect our fellow human beings in every corner of the globe. Whatever affects any one of us affects all of us.

I love the story of Hannah, not least because it leads me through this process of shrinking and growing—that double dynamic of the human story.

Hannah longs for a child. Her longing is so deep that she takes it to God in prayer. Eventually her prayer is answered and she conceives Samuel. So far, this is just a bit of "local news." A woman has conceived a child. It happens all the time—hardly a world-changing matter. No one outside of Hannah's neighborhood would have known or cared about this minor event.

But the birth of a child is always a life-changing event, certainly for the child himself and for his family. Hannah's response is to hand this gift-child over to the Lord, who has given him to her in the first place. The child she has longed for above all else, she now gives back to the Lord. The heartache in this decision can only be imagined. But Hannah's story gives us, perhaps, a little insight into the strange process by which the world can shrink, so that it appears totally within our reach, and yet at the same time challenges our minds and hearts to expand to contain it.

In the birth of her son, Hannah, like all new parents, becomes totally focused on the new life in her arms. All creation, it might feel, is gathered here in this one tiny new being, and all her own energies are directed into caring for him. She suckles him and weans him, and then gives him back to the world and to the Creator of that world. And then the growing begins! Every year, we learn, she goes back to the temple, taking Samuel a new coat. It would be so easy to forget, amid all the temple rituals, that this is a little human being who will grow out of his coat every year. A mother doesn't forget! She deals with the problem. And we can imagine the little boy bursting out of each outgrown coat, and then losing himself in the new one that, like a school outfit at the start of the new school year, was probably way too big for him.

This incident, tucked away in the history of the people of Israel, reminds me that I too need new mental and spiritual "clothes" each year. I grow out of my mind-sets just as a child grows out of his clothes. Every time a bit more of the world, its people, and their concerns comes to my attention, my mind-set has to grow in order to respond to the new challenges that come with them. I find that I can rarely respond fully to tomorrow's problems using yesterday's mind-set. Fortunately God does for us what Hannah does for Samuel. The Creator waits patiently, holding each new coat for us until we are ready to grow into it—which means, of course, that we have to let go of the outgrown mind-set, a process that isn't always painless.

"His mother used to make for him a little robe and take it to him each year."

Look back over any significant growth spurts in your own life, and remember how it felt to let go of outgrown mind-sets in order to be clothed in a bigger way of looking at things. Is there a change like this around in your life right now?

Lord, I know that my mind-set is way too small, but I'm afraid to let go of it. Please ease me into my new and bigger one that will give me space to grow. Amen.

Readiness

Read Matthew 25:1-13.

To wait in wisdom is to wait in a state of readiness. The very
phrase *a state of readiness* can fill our hearts with dread, living as we do in such a dangerous world, where readiness is so
often equated with the availability of firepower and the machin-
ery of destruction. It conjures up images of "red alert," where the
worst is expected and an atmosphere of fear prevails. Surely this
is not the kind of readiness Jesus is urging in this parable.

I remember a startling encounter with readiness that happened
when I was in my early teens. With a school friend of my own
age, I had been preparing for confirmation. The day came, and
we walked together to the altar and knelt to receive the sacra-
ment of confirmation and to make our first Holy Communion.
Not long afterward, my friend became seriously ill with leukemia
and died at the age of fifteen. Amid the shock and disbelief that
such a promising young life had been snuffed out so suddenly, I
remember our vicar's words to me: "She was ready to die." I was
appalled. But over time I came to realize that he was right. He
had seen something of her soul that had been hidden from me.
He had known her with just a little of the knowledge God has of
her. And the more I reflected on his words, the more clear it
became to me that Madeleine had indeed already been living in
a depth of peace that one rarely sees in one so young. She had
known, instinctively, how to "trim her lamp," and there was plenty
of oil in the depths of her heart. When the bridegroom arrived

for her, she was ready. She followed him gladly, and there was a strange joy amid the sorrow. The reflection of that light has continued to accompany me and often to show me the way through the many years that have intervened.

So what kind of a "lamp" are we being asked to trim? What does this readiness mean for us at a personal level?

I had the privilege of spending a quiet day once in a lovely old house whose owners use their home as a retreat for others seeking the stillness of prayer. They themselves are people who live in that state of readiness that was so characteristic of my friend Madeleine. The lamp of their love is constantly aglow, waiting to leap into a powerful flame when it is needed by persons who have lost themselves in the dark of pain or sorrow or confusion. They say little. They listen deeply. They are simply a loving presence to all comers. So it was that I settled into the room they had lovingly prepared for me, and the first thing I noticed was a little oil lamp and a box of matches. I lit the lamp and watched the flame burn steadily, but my gaze soon followed the wick down to the oil in the glass base of the lamp. Not for the first time in my life I felt that God was spelling out to my slow mind something that was abundantly obvious, but that I hadn't really understood until I saw it embodied in this little lamp: The wick will only burn at one end if the other end remains dipped in the oil.

An oil lamp is a powerful metaphor of readiness. We become ready for closer union with God and with one another to the extent that the base of our "wick"—the core of our being—remains submerged in the oil. And we become ready to give light in the world to the extent that the visible end of our "wick" stretches out into that world, sharing in all its hardships and concerns. As long as this is the case, the oil of God's presence will rise steadily through our whole being and turn into our own kind of light for the world. If this connection is broken, our light will flicker and fail.

The process is silent and unseen. God rises through our living in ways we cannot perceive or understand. And each of us must find our own way both of staying immersed in the oil and of being present to the concerns of the world. We stay in the oil through the practice of prayer, whatever form that may take. We burn in the world through the nurturing of deep and loving relationships with other people and with all creation, and through our striving for justice and peace. Without the oil of God's constant presence there can be no flame of action in the visible world.

We can't draw this life-giving energy from anywhere but the oil of our own personal relationship with God. There are no "five wise bridesmaids" sitting alongside who will fill up our lamp from their own supplies. This parable reminds us that it is our own responsibility, as well as our joy, to keep our wicks immersed in God. When we do, the flame will burn in a world that is longing for light and warmth.

"The wise took flasks of oil with their lamps."

Spend a few moments reflecting on your own life's lamp. In what ways is its flame burning and giving light to the world? Where is the source of that energy, the oil? How do you personally ensure that your wick remains immersed in the oil of God's presence?

Lord, "give me oil in my lamp, keep me burning." Let me live in the readiness that comes from your constant love. Amen.

Suffering

Read Mark 5:25-34.

Humanity has struggled through the centuries with the question of suffering. Is it something intrinsically evil that we should do everything to eradicate? Is it something potentially redemptive that takes us deep into the core of our being, in search of healing? Is it something we have to live with—or fight against? Or does the paradox of suffering, perhaps, include elements of all these things?

The woman in today's story has lived for twelve years with a debilitating condition. Her continual hemorrhaging has drained her of all her life energy. It has also rendered her ritually unclean under Jewish law, and condemned her into the role of outcast. But with her last ounce of energy she seeks out Jesus, trusting implicitly that merely to touch the hem of this man's garment will bring her healing.

This story always reminds me of a time in my own life when I was struggling with difficulties that seemed to offer no hope of any improvement. Like the woman in the story, I had invested a lot of time and energy in seeking help, but to no avail. When I recall this experience, I can empathize with the woman's desperation. Perhaps you too have memories of being in a place where there seemed to be no hope of an end to a particular kind of suffering you were enduring.

I remember especially one morning when I hit a low point. Everything suddenly overwhelmed me in a wave of pain and tears, but at the same time I had been reflecting, somewhere in the depths of my heart, on this story of the woman with the hemorrhage. Somehow, that morning, these two facts came together. All I know is that I fell into a deep sleep through sheer exhaustion, and when I woke I felt deeply refreshed, as though in my sleep I too had touched the hem of the Lord's garment. I share this story only in the hope that it might trigger your own memories of when you have "touched the Lord's garment" yourself. That touch may have taken any number of forms. It may have been a moment of desperate vocal prayer or the act of turning to someone else in your need. Jesus can touch us through another's love. His hands are our hands now, and the hem of our garments can be the hem of his, if we are willing to let him live in us and through us.

But the incident is not quite as straightforward as it appears. Jesus is as deeply affected by the woman's touch as she is herself. He knows that they have encountered each other at the most profound level, and he knows that this encounter needs to be openly acknowledged. There has been an exchange of energy between them—and exchange of her suffering for his strength.

In a moving story by Walter Wangerin, Jesus is described as a Ragman who trundles through the world offering "new rags for old."[1] As he meets one suffering person after another, the Ragman takes away the rags of suffering—bloodstained bandages, masks of pain, blankets of despair—and gives the sufferer new clothing. But these are not simply "healing miracles." They are acts of exchange, because, while each sufferer is healed and renewed, the Ragman himself takes on their suffering in his own life, until at last, overwhelmed by the weight of the world's pain, he dies alone on a landfill site. The story leads to resurrection, however, on the other side of death, and it holds the implicit call to each of us to live the Ragman's ministry in our own small way. It calls us to engage with the suffering of one another, risking the exposure to pain we would rather avoid, allowing the sufferer to touch the hem of our garment and trusting that God will use the encounter to bring new life.

The woman's suffering in today's story becomes her personal gateway to God. If she had not been in pain, she might never have encountered Jesus in the crowd. Through her suffering and her desperate need, she meets him in an intimacy she could never have dared to imagine. That intimacy demands an openness and truthfulness that reveals her in all her vulnerability to herself, to the crowd, and to God. It challenges her to say, simply, "Jesus, take me as I am!"

Our bodies and minds have their own God-given wisdom that tells them when they need to reach out to God for healing and restoration. It is our suffering that brings us to the point of such an encounter. When this happens, our lives engage in the amazing and continuous exchange of God's wholeness for our brokenness, God's love for our pain.

"If I but touch his clothes, I will be made well."

Can you recall any moments in your own life when some personal suffering became too much to bear? Perhaps, in your own way, you reached out then to "touch the hem of Jesus' garment." If so, what form did that touch take, and how did God respond? Remember, with gratitude, any human help that was given at that time.

Remembering this experience, be open to the possibility that any pain you may experience in the future, either in body or in mind, is potentially another gateway to God and a new opening to a greater fullness of life in God.

Lord, I would do anything to avoid the pain in my life,
and even the pain in other people's lives. Please give me the
courage to enter into suffering not just as a place of darkness
but as a gateway of possibility, where I can meet you, touch
you, and receive your healing love. Amen.

1. Walter Wangerin Jr., *Ragman: And Other Cries of Faith* (San Francisco: HarperSanFrancisco, 1994).

Recognition

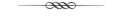

Read Luke 1:39-45.

Yesterday's window opened up into a place of pain and unease—a place where we need to say, "No! I can't take any more!" but lit by the possibility that our experience of suffering may be God's invitation to us to bring deep-buried issues into the light of God's healing love.

Today's window opens us to a different possibility—the possibility of recognizing an indestructible truth and knowledge in the core of our being. It is about the swell of joy, the thrill of "Yes!" that we sometimes experience when something in the ground of our own being has touched something in the ground of another person's being. The resulting resonance is part of God's eternal harmony. We know it, and we long to sing it!

A piece of folk wisdom tells of a person who was asked to look out of a clear glass window and describe what she saw. "I see the street," she said, "and my fellow human beings going about their business." The same person was then invited to look into a mirror and tell of what she saw. "I see myself," she said. "I see my own reflection." The tale goes on to point out that the mirror differs from the window only in its silver coating, and that often it is our own "silver"—our possessions and wealth, real or merely dreamed of—that causes us to look into the glass pane of life and see only ourselves reflected back.

Mary and Elizabeth certainly do not appear to have been weighed down with "silver." Today, as we share in their meeting, we see two women who look through the "glass" of their encounter and see each other. Even more interestingly, each of them needs the other to remind her of who she really is, so far are they both from being self-obsessed.

I often visit this scene in my prayer and my thoughts. I imagine Mary, in her desperate situation, taking herself off to her older cousin Elizabeth who, she believes, will somehow understand, will accept her condition without raised eyebrows, and will give her refuge while she thinks things through. I imagine the look in her eyes as she greets Elizabeth—an expression of reverence for the older woman, who has also been chosen by God to carry a special child—an expression of expectation and trust that Elizabeth will provide the solid basis of wisdom that she so longs for in her new situation. Elizabeth, on the other hand, looks at Mary with the eyes of love and reveres what she sees, in awe that she should be sought out by the mother of her Lord.

And then that moment occurs when the unborn John leaps in recognition of the unborn Jesus! Even in the womb there is deep recognition.

In the mirror we recognize ourselves. Through the glass of the window we recognize each other. But in the moment of deepest intimacy, when heart lies open to heart, we recognize God in each other. This is not just a historical story between two exceptional women, recounted in scripture. It happens every time we are alongside each other with truly open hearts. When this happens, "deep calls to deep," and we discover that there is resonance with the other person at the core of our being. This leap of the heart toward the heart of the other is the hallmark of real "soul friendship."

I recently had the great privilege of meeting a man—another John—already in his sixties, who has spent the last fifteen or more years caring tirelessly and lovingly for his ailing and elderly parents. This task has taken over his life, leaving him little time or energy for anything else, yet he has done it with joy. Sadly, I met him at his mother's funeral. She had been bedridden for years, in a nursing home, and the nursing staff were vigorous in their praise of how he had visited her every day, sat vigil with her through many a long night, and loved her unceasingly. He phoned me this morning to thank me for going to her funeral! He went on to say how wonderful the staff in the nursing home had been, and how selfless in their care for her. All he could see was the goodness in them. He needed me to hold up the mirror that revealed that same goodness in himself.

It reminded me of Mary and Elizabeth. Each of them could see the goodness in the other. They needed each other to recognize the presence of God in themselves.

May our eyes not rest too long on the mirror of our own reflection, but may our gaze move out, through the windowpane, to see the wonder of all that is "other," beyond our own life's orbit, and to recognize God in the core of that "other."

The windows of our Advent calendar now invite us to come closer, not only to look at but to enter into what we see. As we move into the days surrounding the Lord's birth, our Advent journey changes gear as we respond to the heavenly invitation to "come and see this thing that has come to pass."

"As soon as I heard the sound of your greeting, the child in my womb leaped for joy."

Reflect on any moments in your own life when you have been aware of a deeper recognition of the reality of God coming to birth in another person, and that person's recognition of the reality of God coming to birth in you. Do you have a "soul friend"? If so, you might like to visit him or her and talk about how your journey with God is going.

Lord, please give us the grace to see beyond our own reflection to all that is "other," the wisdom to recognize you in that "other," and the courage to enter lovingly into what we see. Amen.

———∞∞∞———

Entering the Mystery

AS WE COME closer to the festival of Christmas, we join Joseph and Mary on their journey to Bethlehem and allow them to draw us with them into the very heart of the mystery. This is a journey we are called to join in, not to observe from a safe distance.

- The journey will lead us to a deeper understanding of where we belong and how that belonging calls us into new ways of relating to one another and to God (December 22).
- Jesus is conceived in emptiness—an empty, waiting womb. We reflect on our own awareness of the empty spaces in our lives and how they can become containers for God's overflowing grace (December 23).
- We share in the stillness of the Holy Night and seek to meet God in the depths of our own hearts' stillness (December 24).
- God is one of surprises. God gives God's self to us in the surprise of Christmas morning and in every new surprise that awaits us around the next corner (December 25).
- In the stable at Bethlehem, the Light of the world has dawned. To enter into this light is also to see our own shadows revealed, yet we enter it in trust, knowing that the light is always more powerful than the darkness in which it is kindled (December 26).
- We often labor to deliver what we think is a happy Christmas. In the days after Christmas, let us also rest, and with the Child's mother, ponder in our hearts the wonder that is unfolding for us (December 27).
- And finally, the shadows lengthen over Bethlehem, and the tyrant's sword strikes terror. Yet our woundedness can also become our blessing. The bittersweet birth of God in our hearts will bring both the wounding and the blessing, as we enter the mystery and commit ourselves to

carry the light of Christ out into the waiting world (December 28).

Belonging

———— ∞∞ ————

Read Luke 2:1-5 and Genesis 12:1-2.

As a cat lover I appreciated a cat joke I heard recently: "A dog has a master," it said, "but a cat has staff!"

Having been, for more years than I care to remember, one of the staff in attendance on one cat after another, I know just how true that is. We can speak of "dog owners" quite happily, and we know that most dogs are more than happy to "belong" to their owners. To speak of owning a cat, however, is nonsense. Cats *choose* to live with you. They don't allow anyone to own them. *They* decide where they "belong" and to what extent.

Does this have anything to show us about the nature of belonging that today's readings explore?

Joseph, we learn, belongs to Bethlehem, because that is where his forebears are from. He is, as it were, on the electoral register there. And Mary, his betrothed, belongs to him and becomes obligated to register wherever he belongs. The call to Joseph comes from secular authority and invokes the power to demand that he return to Bethlehem so that he can be counted in the census.

Abram belongs in Haran, in Mesopotamia. That is the place where his forebears have led him. The call to Abram comes from God and challenges him to move away from his native land so that the journey to the promised land can begin.

Two different calls, in different ways, about the question of belonging, and both precipitating a world-changing journey.

Probably all of us have a deep desire to belong. Small children accept unquestioningly that they belong to a particular family and place. It gives (or should give) them a sense of safety. Young people tend to find their belonging in their peer group. To fall out of line with one's peers is to risk major insecurity. Adults often satisfy their need to belong by entering into exclusive relationships and by identifying themselves with the job they do or the groups they associate with. All this is fine and necessary, of course. It gives structure and boundaries to our lives.

But the word *belong* is a two-edged sword. It can be about the entirely good and necessary sense of being "at home" in a place, a relationship, or a group; or it can be about possession. It begins with "my house belongs to me" and can move, dangerously, into "you belong to me" (and must therefore submit to my will) and "you belong to our group, and no criticism of that group is allowed."

Joseph experiences these two different aspects of belonging in quick succession. Through his God-given dream, he has begun to understand that he and Mary belong together in this awesome call to bring God's Son to birth, and he has accepted the responsibility that this belonging implies. Very soon afterward, he is called to Bethlehem because the authorities there have certain rights of possession over him. The exercise of those rights causes considerable hardship to the embryonic holy family.

Belonging, in its possessive sense, always seems to limit freedom, forcing us to fit into the mold of the ones who are doing the possessing—making Joseph journey to Bethlehem at the height of Mary's pregnancy, making us conform to another person's demands, making us toe the party line. The one who "possesses" may use that power wisely or maliciously, but it remains a question of power.

God's view of belonging seems to be more about relationship than possession. It calls us into greater freedom, if we dare to respond. Joseph is called into full and loving relationship with

Mary and her unborn child. Abram is called into a fuller relationship with God and God's people. This kind of belonging is not about power, but about a desire to commit ourselves in trust to live in a new kind of relationship. It doesn't compel us—it is something we are invited to choose.

When we make a choice to enter into this radical kind of belonging, we enter upon a journey of mystery. We have no idea, for example, what life will bring when we enter into a committed relationship with another human being. We commit ourselves to belong together through thick and thin. To commit ourselves to follow the promptings of God into the unknown is an even more mysterious undertaking. For Joseph and Mary, as for Abram, this new relationship leads to a journey fraught with risk and hardship, taking them far away from the "fixed abode" of their earlier securities and certainties.

If we choose to be in personal relationship with God, we may discover that the only place we can really feel we belong is to the journey itself—the journey into the depths of the mystery we call God.

"Go from your country . . . to the land that I will show you."

Is there any belonging of the possessive kind in your life? Does any individual or group have a possessive hold over you? If so, how do you feel about it?

What relationships have you freely chosen as your places of belonging? What journeys have they led you into? How do you feel about where those journeys are leading?

Lord, to belong to you is to find my home only in the journey that leads into your mystery. Please give me the courage to embrace the challenge of that journey. Amen.

Emptiness

Read Luke 2:6-7; Matthew 8:18-20; and Psalm 114:7-8.

There was a touching little news item not long ago on television about a rabbit who had been rendered homeless because the pregnant family cat had taken over his hutch and set it up as a nursery for her forthcoming litter of kittens. The TV cameras zoomed in to reveal a rather unhappy and bewildered bunny and a very satisfied cat curled up in the hutch, suckling her young family.

The nesting instinct makes itself felt during pregnancy in many different ways. Most mothers-to-be feel a nudge somewhere inside to take some steps to prepare a place for the coming child to be welcomed into the home. Bedrooms are decorated and cribs installed. Soft toys are chosen, and tiny baby clothes are laid out in readiness. The instinct is strong. If necessary, the mother-to-be will make great sacrifices to furnish a nest for the child. It is the beginning of a long period of cherishing and protecting the new generation. And Jesus reminds us that this instinct extends through all the natural world. Foxes have holes; birds build nests. Every creature knows, in its own way, how to make empty, neutral space into a home.

Yet when God is born among us, there is no nest. Instead, Mary spends the final weeks of her pregnancy trekking to Bethlehem, jogged and jostled on the rough back of a donkey. The journey that began in trust leads ever more threateningly into the unknown. Will there be anywhere to stay in Bethlehem? Will there be somewhere warm and sheltered to give birth? The questions must have teemed through her mind as they traveled on.

Of course, we know the answer was "No!" For God, there was only the most makeshift and temporary of nests—in a manger, not in the living space of the inn, but in the part where the animals were kept. And we, whom Jesus calls his brothers and sisters, can expect no more as we make our journey through life in his company.

And it seems to matter to God that God's Son finds only empty space where there should be "home." You may know the story of the little boy who had been chosen to play the part of the innkeeper in the nativity play. When Mary and Joseph knocked at his door, he felt so sorry for them that he changed the script and said, "Come on in; you can have my bedroom!" Our hearts want to say that too. And it's easy to say it in the quiet of our prayer or in the exuberant singing of Christmas carols. It's much harder when we meet God in the terrified faces of our nation's "enemy," or in the hopeless expression of the asylum seeker, or in the young person sleeping in a cardboard box on the city sidewalk. Because to say to them, "Come on in; you can have my bedroom" would mean that we would have to move out! We would have to make space for them by surrendering our own space and risking an unthinkable emptiness.

But the third reading today gives me real hope. God, it reminds us, turns rocks into pools, and flint into fountains. I don't need to search far for the evidence of this fact. The British countryside is full of lakes and ponds, and our hillsides are alive with waterfalls. And these lovely places depend for their very existence on the presence of an empty space where the water can gather, or where the flow of the stream can break through. Emptiness, not fullness, is the secret of these blessings.

When I take these reflections into my own life, I find exactly the same kind of truth. The grace of God has found space in my life in the empty, hollowed-out spaces in my heart, not in the parts of my life that I have managed to fill up with my own "achievements." The fountains of God's love have become real and effective where my own defenses broke down. My breakdowns became God's breakthroughs.

The hollowing out of these spaces has often been painful and heartbreaking, and I would have avoided it if I had seen it coming. Yet now, in hindsight, I can come to these pools and drink deeply from a strength and a love I could never have imagined possible.

God chose an empty space in which to make a nest for Jesus— a virgin's womb. And God prepared that nest by emptying it even further. Mary and Joseph, who began with nothing, lose even their home base and their security en route to Bethlehem. Yet the more deeply their lives are hollowed out, the more grace can flow into the emptiness—grace that will overflow and flood all the world with God's love.

"There was no place for them in the inn."

When you look back over the most important things that have shaped your life, do you find that they grew out of your own fullness or an inner emptiness? Can you see any hollows in your experience that may well have been carved out of you in pain, but have become containers of grace?

Lord, sometimes all I have to bring you are my empty hollows and the flint of my pain. Fill my emptiness, I beg you, with your love, and break through my hard rock in waterfalls of love, overflowing to your thirsty world. Amen.

Stillness

Read John 1:14.

W hen peaceful silence lay over all, and night had run half of her swift course, down from the heavens, from the royal throne, leapt your all-powerful Word" (Wisdom 18:14–15, JB). It is a cold December night as I walk across the Bornholmer Brücke—a humpbacked bridge that connects the former East Berlin to the former West, arching awkwardly over the inner-city railway lines. The frost is sharp, and a layer of Christmas snow encrusts the streets, squeaking beneath my feet, at 5 degrees. The moon rides high in the black of the night—a perfect half-moon. The clean lines of its silver hemisphere might have been cut with a knife. Half a moon and a broken-backed bridge, halfway through the night, at the turning of a year.

The night is vivid for me for other reasons too. For several years I lived in a near-derelict tenement block just the other side of this bridge. I remember how I sometimes walked up to the frontier and watched the bristling guards watching me—how I shielded my eyes against the flare of the searchlights that were combing and roving the no-man's land with predatory malice, demonic mockeries of the silver moonlight.

The city is free now, and this bridge that once divided it reconnects its severed halves. The streets have calmed down, as the last shopping day before Christmas slips away. The buildings of the former East still look dark and drab as they did when the Berlin Wall came down. I lived here in the 1960s, when the Wall was new and sinister and hated. Passing then, between East and West across the checkpoint, had been as stark and sharp as a knife cut. I had functioned at that time as a thin and fragile vein, tenuously connecting the severed limbs of the family by virtue of my foreign passport that opened the borders for me, albeit creakingly.

Then half the city had struggled in a bleak darkness, and the other half had teemed in a bright but garish commercial light. But now it was different. The buildings might still look dark and drab here in the East, but the Western culture has rained down its neon lights and satellite dishes and fast-food chains over the grayness, like cheap tinsel on a dark, brooding pine tree.

It had been a long, dark night, running its course not swiftly but interminably and bloodily, a focal point of European history. The bridge's broken back had been an image in iron of a people's broken connections and their aching pain, their own backs arched in impotent anger. None of us then had truly believed we would see the day when the Wall would fall. Everyone believed that it would surely happen sometime, like the Second Coming, but no one expected it. When we woke up each morning, we never thought, *Maybe today?* We adjusted our dreams and our visions to the lack of freedom, peace, and justice, instead of adjusting our world to embody our dreams and visions.

The tide turned suddenly, while no one was looking. The wind of change blew up like a freak storm, whipping up our unspoken desires until the collective whisper grew into a rumbling and a roar: "You call us the People's Republic. But *we* are the people!" It was a powerful word, wielded without force, springing out of a smothered silence, leaping out of the free spirit of humankind to challenge the darkness. No one who knows this city will ever forget the day that freedom pierced the darkness, like a bolt from the blue, and made the first breach in the Wall that had seemed so permanent. It came so suddenly, so utterly surprisingly, like a baby in a stable, so vulnerable, beneath a cold, shining moon. "When night had run half of her swift course . . ."

From a distant clock tower, I hear the stroke of midnight. The world is still journeying through a long, dark night, and there is a long way to go before daybreak as together we labor to bring God to birth in our darkest human situations. But as I stand here, it is the bright half of the moon I see, not the dark side, and it is the stillness that fills my heart, not the heavy hooves of history. I hear a Word more powerful than all our revolutions, yet gentler than a baby's sigh. A Word with the power, and the desire, to leap from mystery into history and turn the world's course away from darkness and into the radiance of God's dream.

"Peaceful silence lay over all."

Take five minutes today to be perfectly still. The Christ is born into our hearts' stillness, not just today but every moment. He is the turning point of all our nights. Be still and know that he is God.

The night has been lonely, Lord, and the way has been long.
Open our eyes tonight to hear your eternal Word, entering
the midnight silence of our human story. Amen.

Surprises

Read Luke 2:8-18.

T he company that could manufacture joy and market it in person-sized packages would sweep the board. Many have tried and failed. At this time of the year especially, everyone is searching for the magic formula to make this day joyful. During the past few weeks, or even months, we have been inundated by advertising. It's very hard to escape the conclusion that if we spend enough money, consume enough food and drink, and arrange for the right combination of people to share our Christmas table, all will be well.

Yet we know that it isn't always so. Christmas sees the highest prevalence of suicide in the year. Many, many people simply dread the approach of the holiday season, and even those who do have families and friends with whom to share the festivities sometimes find, the day after Christmas, that they are tense and exhausted and feel that they simply tried too hard and are relieved that "It's all over for another year."

Yet this is the day, above all, when God gives joy to the world! What was it that the shepherds understood but eludes us today? What are we missing? We who try so very hard and with genuine goodwill to make Christmas a special day all too often miss out on the joy it is supposed to bring. The shepherds weren't trying at all. For them it was just another night on the hillside, getting on with their routine work. The whole thing took them completely by surprise.

It begins with a surprise visit! The last thing the shepherds were expecting on a cold night out on the hillside was a visit from the heavenly hosts. Surprise visits are a mixed blessing at the best of times, perhaps especially at Christmas. They are so much a part of what Christmas is about, and with our lips at least, we welcome them. "Why don't you drop by for a visit?" we invite the neighbors genially but secretly hope they will come at the "right" time and not outstay their welcome. The angels didn't wait to be invited. The news they had was so momentous that there was no way it could wait until the invitation cards had been printed. And it called forth a response in the shepherds that went a good deal further than a piece of pie and a cup of coffee. Perhaps because they were themselves at the bottom of the social heap, with no image to defend, they seem to have been amazingly open to the angels' message, once they had overcome their initial shock—so open that they immediately set off to make a surprise visit themselves to the little family in Bethlehem.

We can only imagine the reaction of Mary and Joseph to the sudden arrival of these unexpected guests! No chance to clean up the stable or bake a cake. "You'll have to take us as you find us!" we sometimes warn our would-be guests, which, for me at least, is usually an excuse for being too lazy to clean the house. God says the same, but from a higher motive. "Come and look for me where you least expect me, and then be prepared to take me as you find me!" Where will we find God this Christmas? Certainly in the hospitality of our friends. But perhaps more visibly and powerfully in the faces of those who have no home, no friends, no resources behind which to hide their extreme vulnerability. A surprise visit to such a person would perhaps surprise us with the warmth it would generate.

Surprises are the very essence of Christmas morning. All those gifts we have carefully concealed are joyfully unwrapped. Those with children will be bombarded today with demands to "Look!" and to join in with the new games, admire the new doll, share in the joy. Surprises are for sharing. The bigger the surprise, the less it can be contained. And all our unwrapping and our sharing is just a faint reflection of God's own great act of unwrapping God's self to reveal a helpless baby in the arms of two inexperienced parents. It was the mother and father of all surprises. No wonder the shepherds ran off to tell everyone they met about the amazing events of an "ordinary" night.

"All who heard it were amazed."

The vulnerable baby who is God's own self has countless siblings. Some of them live in your neighborhood. You will recognize them because they are a gift that comes unwrapped, with the eyes of need looking straight into your own—a single parent, a bewildered immigrant, a lonely senior adult. Why not plan to surprise one of them with a touch of God's love this Christmas season? You might be surprised at the results!

Lord, your gift to us of your very self still lies, unwrapped, in the forgotten corners of our world. Give us, today, the joy of rediscovering your presence in the presence of one another. Amen.

Light

⎯⎯⎯ ∞∞ ⎯⎯⎯

Read John 1:1-5, 9-12.

W hen our daughter was born, one of the first difficulties we encountered was the problem of light. To make sure that she would always experience the presence of a gentle, comforting light if she awoke during the night, we installed a little lamp close to the nursery door. It also meant that if she cried we could grope our way to her even in a half-asleep state.

However, visits to a newborn baby in the night can be frequent and can take a heavy toll on the parents' mental and physical well-being. One of the side effects of surviving on a meager ration of sleep is that the eyes start to burn. Even the little nursery light, we soon discovered, burned our eyes, especially after the third or fourth unscheduled awakening during the night. So we went to the local electrical shop to ask whether they had any bulbs lower than 15 watts!

It's strange how light that is so needful for growth and life can also be so hurtful when we are unprepared for it.

The beautiful prologue to John's Gospel speaks of how God's word first brings life into being, and we can almost picture the dawn of creation in his description of a life that springs from God's word and brings light into a dark void. Such immensity lies beyond our imagination, but we can rediscover the awesomeness of this first creating word simply by noticing the gradual growth of something as tiny as a seed. In the winter season the seeds are deep in the darkness of the earth, yet as winter gradually releases its grip, they begin to respond to a light they cannot yet perceive. Deep in the earth they begin to grow. As the strength of daylight increases and spring approaches, they will eventually break the surface of the soil and grow to become the plants and flowers we recognize and love.

If they could talk, they would perhaps tell us of the joy and comfort they discover in the gentle light of spring, much as, we hope, our little daughter found comfort in the nursery lamp. But the light increases with every passing day. Summer comes and the flowers are exposed to a light with the power to open up those soft petals to an unpredictable exposure. There will be the joy of blossoming and pollination, but the fierce rays of sunlight will eventually wither the flower and release the seeds of next year's growth. Every new life likewise faces the light that brings joy, and the light that burns and exposes. Our own lives are no exception.

But we can be so fearful of the light that exposes that we try to hide away from the light that brings life and growth. The seed of God falls into the darkness of our hearts and grows, but the darkness in which it grows feels threatened by it and seeks to suppress or even destroy it, for as T. S. Eliot says, "Humankind cannot bear too much reality."

And so the very light that we long for in the hours of our darkness is the same light that we want to dim because it burns our hearts too much. Perhaps we fear that God's candle in our nursery might become the fierce beam of the interrogator's light, exposing all our darkness. But what if this light, whose glare we so dread, were the beam of the surgeon's light, searching out our need for healing? What if it were the light that releases all our fruitfulness, even as it withers our petals?

But God's light is gentle. For most of us it will grow like the light of springtime, coaxing us out of our darkness. It begins with the 15-watt bulb, as the desire for life and for God gradually awakens in us, and it takes us steadily forward until we are ready for a stronger beam. Let us not say "No" in fear to what our hearts most desire, for to dim God's light in our hearts is to subdue life itself.

"The light shines in the darkness, and darkness did not overcome it."

In a quiet moment, after dark, switch off all the lights and light a candle. What happens to the darkness as soon as you light the candle? What happens to the candlelight? Does the darkness put it out?

Now apply the same logic to any situation in your own life that feels dark. Is there anything you can do, however small, to "light a candle" in that dark situation—perhaps a calm conversation, a letter, a gesture of reconciliation, a word of challenge? Can you trust that such a candle will also have more power than all the darkness around it?

Lord, I bring you the darkest place in my experience right now, and I ask you to steady my hand as together we light a candle that will banish the power of darkness forever. Amen.

Resting

Read Matthew 11:25-30 and Luke 2:19-20.

The festivities are over, and perhaps we are back to cold turkey. For many of us, a rest is called for after a strenuous few days. For the new parents in Bethlehem, any rest they might have been able to find after the events of the weeks leading up to the birth of Jesus was to be short-lived, but for today, let's join them in the calm of the stable lodgings. Their son was to become the one who would promise to give them—and us—rest for our souls. He was the one who would teach us all that God reveals the secrets of God's mystery to children and to the unlettered, more easily than to those who have the degrees and the certificates. But for today, we find him simply lying in his mother's arms. And we find his parents simply resting in their joy that he has come into the world.

In our more "advanced" world, such rest might well have been denied to Mary in the name of medical progress. My own "recovery time" after my daughter's birth was one long round of doing whatever was on the hospital's agenda at any given time. The day began at six in the morning, and there was no respite until night—except, that is, at visiting time. When visitors showed up at the doors, we were hastily shunted into bed, where we were supposed to appear serene and untroubled. I'm not sure whether the hospital got extra brownie points for presenting such a placid set of new mothers to the eyes of the anxious visitors. I only know that I didn't get a moment's rest until I arrived home again. And it was then that nature compelled me, through sheer exhaustion, to spend quality time doing nothing other than simply sitting with my daughter in my arms, letting her be, and learning how to *be* myself.

I pondered deeply during those times, through daytime and nighttime feedings, watching her sleep or waiting for her to awaken. I thought about the world she would grow up in, the person she would become, and what really mattered to me. But most of all, I enjoyed those times. With hindsight I can say that I felt closer to the mystery of God, holding this little child, than I had ever come in long years of studying and trying to work things out.

How, I wonder, did we ever learn the things that are most important to us? I suggest that we learned a lot of them just by being still, sometimes alone, sometimes in another person's embrace, perhaps in the dependency of childhood, perhaps in a time when our own strength gave out and we were forced into passivity. We learn to love by being loved. We learn to trust when our needs are cared for by another. We learn courage and resilience when we come against the hard rock and are compelled to rely on resources deeper than our own. We learn life skills by watching another at work. We learn to listen by being listened to, to be tolerant by being tolerated ourselves. So much of what matters most in life we learn simply by watching, gazing, resting in another's arms; and we learn much of this long before we are old enough to realize that there is anything to learn.

In Britain we use the term *reception class* to describe the first class at school for kindergarteners. Because we tend to believe that we adults, the "wise and the learned," are the ones who have everything to impart to the young, we think of it as the class where we "receive" these five-year-olds into the world of learning. If we could see with God's eyes, we would surely realize that it is the children who are doing the receiving, because they are so receptive. They are receiving the seeds of their own stories just by listening to the world's stories. They are perfectly willing to drop everything just to watch a beetle cross the floor. The clock, mercifully, hasn't yet caught up with them, and they are wide open to everything that creation is waiting to reveal to them. However active their minds and bodies may be, their souls are still at rest.

I spend a great deal of my time running around like a headless chicken, trying to *do* things. When I'm not busy doing, I'm preparing for the next thing that has to be done. It all feels so important, but when I recall those early days when I had nothing to do but hold my child and watch her grow, I know that was my life's most important learning curve.

"Mary treasured all these words and pondered them in her heart."

Take some quality time today just to *be*. Spend a little while watching, gazing, pondering. If there is a child around, or if you have a pet, watch them and let the experience go deep into your heart, or simply be present to the wonder of some aspect of the natural world. Let it connect to other times in your life when you have stopped *doing* for a while and entered the real world of learning, where the mystery of God has opened up to you and taught you something of eternal importance.

Lord, may I find a way today to make it a little easier for someone close to me to take a rest. And then, Lord, may I rest too. Amen.

Blessing

Read Numbers 6:22-27 and Matthew 2:16-18.

Soon after the "Velvet Revolution" that freed the Czech
Republic from totalitarian rule, during the historic collapse
of East European communism in 1989, I was visiting friends in
Prague. They were eager to show me the sights of this beautiful
city, but having lived there all their lives and shared personally
in its sufferings and struggle, they were able to show me places
that lay well off the tourist beat.

In one such place, my hostess drew my attention to a dark
corner of a nondescript road, and tried, in imperfect English, to
explain why this spot was significant. I gathered that some kind
of student uprising had occurred there, but I couldn't figure out,
from what she was telling me, how it had ended.

"The students staged a protest against the regime here," she
told me, "and many of them were blessed."

I couldn't make any sense of this. The idea of some priest
turning up in the middle of a student riot in a communist country to "bless" its victims seemed bizarre. But no amount of questioning or explanation could shed any light upon the matter. We
had to leave it as one of life's unsolved mysteries and accept the
linguistic frustrations.

Only when I was lying in bed that night, still thinking about
this strange incident and the "blessing," did it suddenly occur to
me that my hostess, who spoke several foreign languages, always
chose to use French if she could, as this was her preferred second

language. And the French word *blesser* means "to wound." All became clear in an instant. The student riot had been violently put down, and many of the students had been wounded!

Since then I have often wondered about the unintended connection made that day in my mind between "blessing" and "woundedness." The child who is born in Bethlehem brings God's eternal blessing to a broken world, yet within a very short time of his birth, an atrocity is perpetrated that makes our blood run cold, even at this distance in time. A deadly kinship exists between the massacre of the infants of Bethlehem and the appalling acts of terrorism and "ethnic cleansing" that stalk our world today. The birth of the child who brings blessing also provokes terrible violence. The wounded world strikes back against God's blessing, and thirty-three years later, only the violent death of that same blessed child will turn curse back into blessing.

The massacre at Bethlehem is a stark reminder that this event is not just a cozy nativity scene, where a smiling baby lies on a bed of clean straw, radiant in the starlight. This smiling baby is a Savior. He is a Savior because that, above all, is what the world needs. And he is a Savior who will save and bless us not by an act of transcendent power but by surrendering himself to the very woundedness he comes to heal.

And what of our own woundedness? Can it ever be a blessing? History certainly records many cases of individuals who have found what really mattered to them when they were laid low by injury or illness. There is a folk tale about a tribe who spent all their time and energy searching for the "holy mountain." They ran around in circles, bumping into one another in their efforts to meet their goal. But the only ones who ever found it were those who fell over in all the hustle and bustle. Then, lying helpless on their backs, they would look up and see what their healthy brothers and sisters had missed—the holy mountain!

When I look back over the years of my life, with their successes and their disasters, I know for sure that it was the disasters that drew me closer to God. When I was prone and helpless, I had no option but to acknowledge how much I needed help—to look up and, through my tears, see God's face looking down, blessing me and keeping me, letting the radiance of God's face shine on me, bringing me peace.

"The Lord bless you and keep you."

Remember a time in your own life when you have been wounded, either physically or emotionally. With hindsight, can you see how any blessing flowed from that woundedness? How did that blessing take shape in your life, helping you grow or changing your attitude in any way?

Bring your memories into the stillness of prayer, and for a few minutes do absolutely nothing but sit in the presence of God, letting the warmth of God's love shine through your whole being, like the warmth of a sunlit dawn, bringing you new life.

Lord, the light of your blessing reveals our scars. May our scars lead us into a deeper understanding of your blessing. Amen.

———— ∞∞∞ ————

Windows
Become Doors

THE SUPERMARKETS are stocking up again for the next big shopping spree before New Year's. Is Christmas over for another year, or is it just beginning? Giving birth to a child is one thing, but bringing up that child to maturity is quite another. It is a long-term commitment—a huge challenge and a great joy. The Christ child is born in our hearts. How are we going to make him a reality in our everyday living? At this point in our journey, the windows of our Advent calendar turn into doors, through which we are called out to the waiting world, to turn our believing into loving service.

- Mary and Joseph bring the infant Jesus to the temple to consecrate him to God, and we join them in listening to the words of Simeon, who had been waiting in patience and in trust for this moment (December 29). He opens the first door for us and challenges us to walk through into the world Christ has come to save, risking the sword, trusting the grace.
- We allow Jesus to commission us for the onward journey (December 30).
- We receive Christ's anointing, healing our brokenness and marking us as ones who serve (December 31).
- The onward journey is a journey into transformation—of ourselves and of our world. This transformation is possible only if we are willing to pass through the narrow ways of difficulty and surrender (January 1).
- It is also a journey into freedom. Dare we risk God's liberating power in our lives (January 2)?
- As we journey on, we learn to look for and find God's unfailing nourishment along the way and to drink life-giving water from the unfailing Source of all our energy (January 3).

- Our energy for the journey depends on our staying always rooted in Christ, the vine, and resisting the pervasive human temptation to live by our own strength (January 4).

- The Christmas season is coming to a close, and the postal rush is over, but we ourselves are "letters of Christ," sent out into the world, carrying his love (January 5).

- Finally, like the Magi, we return to the place we came from, but by a different route. We return to where we belong, but we are changed by the journey and we carry the seeds of ongoing change and growth with us. On January 6 we celebrate the coming of the Good News to the whole world, far beyond the land of the nativity.

We have looked into the lighted windows of God's guidance, wisdom, and love. We have entered into the mystery of God's coming to birth, and we are sent back to make God's kingdom a reality in our own place and time.

Revealing

Read Luke 2:22-35.

Simeon's words became imprinted upon my mind at a very early age. I was in the choir of the local parish church as a young schoolgirl, and every Sunday we would sing the words of the Nunc Dimittis during Evensong. I loved the words even then. They brought Sunday to the right kind of close and seemed to bless us on our way into the week ahead.

During these final few days with our Advent calendar, the direction changes. We have allowed its windows to lead us closer and closer to the mystery of God-with-us, and to share something of the joy and blessing of the nativity, but now Simeon reminds us that we are being sent out, back into the world, carrying with us something of the starlight. Simeon reminds God that it's okay for God to let him go, now that he has seen the promised child. What about ourselves? We too, each in our own way, have seen the light of Bethlehem. Is it okay for God to let us go? Are we ready, as Simeon was, to take the next step? For him it was the final passage from mortal to immortal life. For us it is the passage into a new year, full of unknown challenges.

Notice that there are no guarantees. The fact that we have known the touch of God upon our lives is not an insurance policy against anything the world might throw at us in the year ahead. Simeon is under no illusion about what the coming of this child is going to mean. Things are going to get worse, it seems, before they get better. The events of the first Christmas will turn the world upside down, attract opposition, and bring deep personal anguish to those who know the child and love him, starting with his mother. The outlook that Simeon describes is not, on the surface, very appealing. We could be forgiven for saying, "Thank you, but we'll leave things as they are."

So what keeps us with it? Why do we keep on believing and seeking to live out our Christian faith when the prognosis is that we will be challenged to journey through heartbreak as well as through joy?

Perhaps Simeon's encounter with the newborn Christ gives us a clue. For me, this clue lies in the words "My eyes have seen your salvation." My guess is that, for most of us, the reason we keep on traveling the way of Christ is because in some form or other, at some point in our lives, we have known in our own personal experience what it means to feel God's touch upon us. This kind of knowledge doesn't lodge in our heads but in our hearts and in our gut. We know forever what we have ever known, however fleetingly, of how we, individually and uniquely, have encountered God. Such knowledge can never be negated or argued away. Even if all the outer wrappings of our faith—the creeds and doctrines, the words and rituals—were to disappear or be discredited, no one ever could wipe out that deep inner knowledge we possess, that in our own way we too have seen some glimpse of the reality of God, and it has made a life-changing difference to us.

Of course we don't want the sword to pierce our hearts, laying bare our secret thoughts; yet, paradoxically, this is also what we deeply desire, if this is the way in which the kingdom of Christ is coming into being in our world.

"My eyes have seen your salvation."

The direction has turned, and now, having been so deeply drawn into the mystery of God incarnate, we are sent out to live what we have seen and known. The sending out is rooted for each of us in that personal way in which God has revealed God's mystery to our own hearts. Spend a little while reflecting on how God has revealed God's self to you. The revealing may have happened in big turning points or in tiny glimpses of something eternal. What is it in your own spiritual experience that keeps you traveling this way? In what personal way do you feel able to say with Simeon, "My eyes have seen something of your reality, Lord. Now you can let me go, to live out that vision, because I shall never again lose what my heart knows"?

Lord, please open my eyes every new day to see the ways your love is touching my life. Then send me forward into tomorrow to make this love incarnate in your world. Amen.

Commissioning

⎯⎯⎯∞∞∞⎯⎯⎯

Read Luke 4:14-21.

E very now and then, I find myself in a library that houses
thousands of theological books. I cast my eyes along the
shelves and run my fingers across the leather spines of these
imposing volumes, but deep inside, my heart shrinks and recoils.
Can my believing depend on all this stuff? What hope for normal mortals if the brightest brains of the ages have needed miles
of shelf space to explore the complexities of what faith means?

The incident described in today's reading dispels those fears
totally. In just a single sentence, Jesus tells us all we need to know
about the mission we are being invited to engage in.

It's about touching people's lives with hope and encouragement, and giving them real reason to want to go on living, though
their world feels dark and hopeless.

It's about speaking the word that gives freedom—freedom to
be real, to speak from the heart, to go beyond the fear, to risk
breaking out of the old, outgrown molds that society and reli-
gion can set us into.

It's about discovering a deeper layer of vision—of insight—
in situations where we can't see our hands in front of us for the
fog of bewilderment and confusion.

It's about searching for ways to release ourselves and one
another from the oppressions of the twenty-first century—
whether they are the oppressions of political tyranny, poverty
and injustice, or stress and burnout.

And it's about declaring the truth we know in our hearts, that God (and not the power of the market) is the bottom line of everything we call life—that there is a center of gravity beyond ourselves that holds us in being.

We see "mission statements" everywhere around us these days, in the boardrooms of multinational companies and at the entrance to the supermarket! We may or may not be impressed by what we see there, but in today's reading we hear Jesus' own mission statement. It's simple, practical, and it's about relationship with God and with one another. We don't need a degree to understand it, but we do need a grain of humility to try to live it. It calls us to keep our focus firmly on God and on one another in everything we do, and to preface all our decisions and reactions with the questions "How does this relate to God's mission and my role in it? What is the most Christlike thing to do next in this particular situation?"

If I let my imagination run free for a moment, I can almost see Jesus standing up in that theology library, much as he did in the synagogue. I can see him looking with the eyes of wisdom and of love through all those books—all the striving of human minds to find the truth—and spelling out again the simplicity and the challenging profundity of the call to be Christlike in our own circumstances and our own generation. I can hear him distilling into a single sentence all that really matters out of all our searching, and turning to each one of us with these words: "This mission is being fulfilled right now, right where you are, in ways that make a difference to the real world, and you have a role to play in its fulfillment."

Jesus returned to Galilee, to the place where he had been brought up. He proclaimed God's love among the people who had grown up with him, gone to school with him, played in the streets with him. He made God's love incarnate in his genera-

118

tion, for all generations, on his home ground, but for all the earth. When he speaks in his mission statement of the words being fulfilled "today," he means this year, this week, this moment. When he speaks in Nazareth, he speaks in our country, our town, our street. When he speaks, he asks us first to listen and then to go out and live his words in the place where we find ourselves.

We are co-missioners with Christ and for Christ. We are commissioned by him to make his life and values incarnate in our day.

"This scripture has been fulfilled in your hearing."

Take a moment to read through and reflect on the points Jesus mentions in his "mission statement": to bring good news to the afflicted, to set the captives free, to give sight to the blind, to release those who are oppressed, to proclaim God's love in our own way and our own lives.

Notice any of these points that speaks to your heart especially. When has God done this for you? How might God be inviting you to use your own experience and the power of the Holy Spirit to do the same for someone else?

Lord, let your mission live on in me—not in what I know, or even just in what I do, but in who I am, in you. Amen.

Anointing

———— ✦ ————

Read Luke 7:36-50.

I am old enough to remember a coronation. It alarms me to recall that it was half a century ago! At the time, I was a little girl in primary school, and I can vividly remember being considerably more impressed by the prospect of a day off from school than by the pomp and ceremony being displayed on the (then quite rare) television screens. We celebrated that day as a family by making the trek to my grandmother's home in the Lincolnshire countryside. The reason probably had a lot to do with the fact that she possessed one of those rare televisions, and our elders thought it would make a good excuse for a family reunion. I can't even say that I remember seeing much of the proceedings, as no doubt we were supposed to do. But I do remember an exciting day playing with my young cousins in and out of the dikes and hedgerows that characterize that part of the country.

Nevertheless, it's impossible to grow up in a monarchy (even a democratic one) without being aware of the ceremony of the anointing of a crowned head of state. The anointing that takes place in a coronation is an anointing for service, and even as a child, I do remember being moved by the pictures of a very young woman making solemn and heartfelt promises to serve a nation to the best of her ability.

There is something very sacred about the act of anointing. It has been hallowed through all the ages as a symbol of sending out a person to live a life of service for others.

If we are to be sent out into the world to serve others as God has taught us through the life of Jesus, we too will be "anointed" for the task. But we won't go to that anointing in a golden coach, nor will our commissioning be sealed with orb and scepter. If the One we follow is any guide of what to expect, the crown will be of thorns, not of gold, and the symbols of power will become icons of helplessness.

That is why today's story of the unruly intruder into the Pharisees' dinner party appeals to me so much, as a more realistic picture of an anointing. There is a "demon" inside me who revels in this scene and the social disruption it must have caused. The vision of the good and worthy Pharisees, pillars of society, having their aperitifs and hors d'oeuvres interrupted by a woman from the streets sets the scene wonderfully for all that Jesus is going to teach them. This woman has known the touch of Jesus upon her life. The love he has inspired in her is like a bright ball of light that in turn reveals the deep, dark shadows across her life. She brings both of these things—the love and the shame— and anoints Jesus there and then with both tenderness and tears.

Jesus turns the shock-horror reaction of his hosts on its head by reminding them that the measure of our love for him is a reflection not of our worthiness but of our need. We overflow with love when we recognize just how much his touch has healed in us and how desperately we needed that touch. Our response remains politely lukewarm if we imagine that we are making out quite well on our own, though we might occasionally invite him to share an evening with us.

In her own way, this woman is anointing Jesus for the suffering that lies ahead, but paradoxically, he is also anointing her, to love and serve her brothers and sisters with that warm river of love that his touch has opened up in her heart. He asks no less of us.

"She has bathed my feet with her tears and dried them with her hair."

The woman in this scene anoints Jesus with love and tears that flow out of the emptiness and brokenness within her. Take a moment to go into the depths of your own emptiness and brokenness. Don't be afraid to do so, because Jesus himself prays with you and carries you to the darkest recesses of your heart. In that awareness of utter need, anoint him in your own way, either with words or in silence.

Lord, so often I keep you at a safe distance, inviting you into my life only on my own terms. Please unstop the cork of my heart and free me to pour out my deepest longings for your love, even when they carry me beyond the limits of my own control. Amen.

Transforming

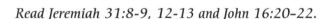

Read Jeremiah 31:8-9, 12-13 and John 16:20-22.

One of my most cherished and abiding memories of childhood is of my mother sitting beside the fire each evening, working patiently at her embroidery. It was always a source of amazement to my teachers at school, when they tried to teach me to sew, that such an incompetent child could have sprung from such a gifted mother. And she really was talented. She loved her work and rejoiced in the beauty that came forth from her needle. Yet her gift was only discovered through need. When my father lost his job and became ill, she had no choice but to look for a way to earn our bread, and she turned to embroidery as her way of keeping our heads above water. When I think of the long, long hours she spent over her work, and the very meager payments she received, I marvel at her patience. But even more than that, I can see how this whole process became, for us, one of God's transforming acts. And the needle gives me a clue about how God transforms.

What turns a single length of thread into a part of a beautiful piece of embroidery? What turns the broken threads of our own experience into living strands of a new creation? When I close my eyes and remember my mother, one answer seems to crystallize before me—"the eye of the needle." I have watched my mother thread her needle thousands of times. I have seen the colored embroidery silks being cut off and threaded through that (for me!) impossibly small eye. And I have seen the results: lovely tablecloths, delicate pictures for framing, lovingly created designs to transform the ordinary into the extraordinary.

The transformation that took place, however, wasn't simply about tablecloths. It was about ourselves as members of a family in difficulties. By her patient labor and her belief in a better future, my mother pulled us through that period as surely and trustfully as she pulled her embroidery silks through the eye of her needle. She had no guarantees, as she sewed, that there would be a market for her work, and she had no conception, as she placed each stitch, that the whole would become something so much greater than the sum of its constituent threads. As I look back on those long-ago years, I see something of God's transforming love there.

Transformation leads from the place of tears to the place of joy, changing mourning into gladness and the agony of childbirth into the joy of new life. But there is no shortcut to transformation. It leads through the eye of the needle, not around it, and it demands trust. Sometimes the place of joy seems to elude us forever, and the eye of the needle seems to be all that there is. The Gethsemane of our pain, and the cold abandonment of Calvary, can tempt us to despair as we struggle to get our life's thread through the narrow "eye" of our circumstances. We can lose all sight and all hope of there ever being a resurrection.

I know now, with the benefit of hindsight, that my mother was trapped in the eye of a needle more sharp and piercing than I, as a child, could ever have guessed. In her own way she was passing through a kind of Calvary, and she made that journey with nothing but love to support her. That was all. That was enough. We came through, but we came through transformed. We learned about patience and resilience. We grew, individually and as a family, from our experience.

It all helps to convince me that God's transformation happens when we embrace the "eye of the needle," whatever form that may take in our living. We miss out on it every time we try to avoid the constriction of the "narrow way." We grow beyond it every time we allow God to draw us through our crisis times on the thread of God's unconditional love.

"You will have pain, but your pain will turn into joy."

Reflect for a while on any "narrow ways" through which your own life has led. How did it feel for you at the time, as you passed through the time of difficulty? Can you see any evidence of transformation as a result of your experience? How did it change you?

Lord, please take the broken and separated threads of our own experience and transform them into the tapestry of your kingdom. Amen.

Liberating

Read Acts 12:1-16 and Psalm 124:7.

I used to work in a high-rise office building and, like all my colleagues, I needed a magnetic ID card to access any of the offices. One morning I arrived at work, took the elevator up to the tenth floor where I was based, and slipped my card through the magnetic reader fixed beside the door. Nothing happened! Frustrated, I tried again and again, only to be greeted by an unblinking red light that, for me, said that either the whole system had frozen up or there was something amiss with my own card. Either way, there seemed to be no way of getting to my desk. I began to wonder whether to go home again or settle myself out there in the lobby for the day. But by way of one last desperate effort, I waved frantically to attract the attention of my colleagues who were getting on with their work on the other side of the closed door, apparently unconcerned about my predicament or the vagaries of the security system.

Eventually one of them noticed me, came ambling across to the door, which he nonchalantly opened, and greeted me with the question, "What's your problem, Margaret? The door's open. All you needed to do was turn the handle and come in!"

I discovered that the security locking system had failed that day, and all the access doors in the building were behaving like normal doors for once, instead of like portals to Fort Knox. I felt every kind of a fool as I walked to my desk, greeted by the friendly laughter of my workmates.

So I can feel for poor Rhoda! There they all are, praying fervently for Peter's release from captivity, but when the man actually arrives and knocks at the door, no one can believe the evidence of their eyes. So they leave him standing there while they try to rationalize this unexpected turn of events. "You must be seeing things," they tell Rhoda. "It must be some kind of apparition."

Why is the obvious so difficult to accept? Why wasn't my first thought to assume that the door was open until proved otherwise? Why didn't Rhoda let Peter in and believe in his liberation?

God must get so frustrated at our obtuseness and our inability to let God be God. Just as I tried to place the misbehaving door into the only category I knew—which was "locked"—so these first Christians placed God's liberating miracle into the only category they understood, which was "impossible." As long as we insist on remaining in our closed boxes of limited understanding, God's liberating love can be blocked. And as long as we insist on remaining in cages that our own mind-sets have manufactured, we won't be able to walk free into God's tomorrow.

"The chains fell off his wrists."

God's freedom can be so much easier than we dare imagine, if we let God free us from the mind-set that convinces us we are captive in particular situations.

Is there any situation in your own life where you feel imprisoned? If so, talk it through with the Lord in your prayer, and ask God to open your eyes and your mind to "try the door." It may open more readily than you think. Sometimes just a slight shift of attitude or expectation can move an intractable situation forward so that new growth can begin.

Lord, nothing so entraps us as our own conviction that we are prisoners. Please give us the courage and the confidence to "try the doors" of our life's prisons, and the wisdom to shift our thinking just enough to let a little light into our own places of darkness. Amen.

Nourishing

Read Exodus 16:2-4, 11-16, 19.

The complaining of the children of Israel needs no translation! We know the tones of petulance in our own living and journeying. Few of us will not at some time have thrown our reproaches at God. "Why did I ever set out on this Christian journey? I could have had a far less demanding life if I'd simply stayed put and got on with the task of building up my own little kingdom. Becoming a coworker for your kingdom sometimes seems to be a path to nowhere!"

We often hear the word *burnout* used in the context of Christian ministry. I used to think it was something of an overstatement until I started to experience its symptoms myself. Now I realize all too well that it is possible to become so drained of energy and so starved of personal nourishment that it is tempting to sit down and abandon the journey altogether. What keeps us going when we feel like that? Where do we find new energy? How do we refuel?

When I reflect on my own need for nourishment, I find two kinds of energy sources in my life—renewable and nonrenewable. Most of the time I try to keep on filling up from the nonrenewable sources. I read books, attend courses, and try to harvest knowledge and experience. I look for energy and renewal by eating well—sometimes too well! I even try to draw my energy from other people, imposing unreasonable expectations upon them to inspire, enthuse, or comfort me. When I look at these strategies for keeping going, I begin to see that my own life can become something rather like a marathon motorway journey, a frenzied sequence of activity punctuated by emergency stops at the fuel pumps, where I drain the planet a little more of its energy reserves. The fact that some of my frenzied activity is "for the Lord" doesn't prevent my running dry on a regular basis.

Every now and then I sit down to reflect on what really does give me real energy and nourishment on my journey. And I discover, to my surprise, that there is a very real and trustworthy source of renewable energy. Renewable energy comes straight from the source of all energy, who is God. It can be drawn upon in times of silence, stillness, and prayer. But it also comes in wholly unexpected encounters with God's surprises.

We all have probably been down the track of "Sorry, Lord, no time to pray today. Too busy. Wish you were here!" And off we go into the day's whirlwind, knowing full well, if we stop to think, that we will run dry by lunchtime and need an energy boost from somewhere or someone. We will "snack" on this kind of fast food, even though it has been borrowed, or even stolen, at the expense of someone else. It has come from nonrenewable sources.

God offers us another way. God invites us to spend quality time drinking from the deep, eternal wells of divine presence in prayer. And God gives us a whole variety of nourishment "in flight" as well. The story of the manna in the desert helps me to rediscover God's ways of feeding me, and to receive my "daily bread" in a new kind of way.

Yesterday, for example, disappeared into a haze of hyperactivity: an early start, a retreat to facilitate, a number of people to meet in one-to-one conversations. The day ended with a four-hour drive home along crowded motorways, in drizzling rain. Yet when I reflected back over the day, I recognized my "manna and quails." A Communion service celebrated with such sensitivity and tenderness that I had tears in my eyes as I received the consecrated bread. A story shared by someone who entrusted me with her own "pearl of great price" and allowed us to marvel together at its uniqueness. A city executive who opened up his own deep vulnerability to find a deeper strength in his weakness. The picture and words on a thank-you card that made my heart swell with love. The list goes on. At the end of the day I had not only been adequately nourished, I had been given a feast, and none of it had been taken at the expense of another. It had all come from the renewable source of all energy, who is God.

We can't store up the nourishment that we really need. We have to take it on trust. We have to become like babies at the breast, not fretting about tomorrow's needs but enjoying today's supply. Perhaps this is the only reliable antidote to burnout.

"I am going to rain bread from heaven for you."

Look back over the past twenty-four hours. How has God nourished you from God's eternally renewable sources? What form did your "manna" take? Express your gratitude to God in your own way.

Lord, I am hungry, and the food I take from the world continually runs out. Teach me to drink from your wells, to discover your manna each day, and to share this eternal nourishment with those around me. Amen.

Empowering

Read John 15:1-5, 15-17.

My favorite childhood playground was the woods at the back of our home. Whenever I wanted to, I could slip through a gap in the fence and enter those woods; I especially enjoyed doing this during the springtime, when the woods were thickly carpeted with bluebells. Sometimes the overwhelming sea of blue was so desirable that I couldn't resist the urge to gather an armful of the flowers and take them home. When I did so, inevitably and sadly, they would start to wilt before evening came. Perhaps this was my first lesson about allowing creation to remain whole, and not trying to take one part of it for my own purposes. The part that is separated dies. The wholeness continues to flourish.

As I grew older, I began to do my "bluebell picking" in even more damaging ways. I bought into the illusion that I was somehow self-sufficient—an illusion that our Western culture particularly tries to sell us. I frequently took the part I wanted at the expense of the wholeness I really needed. I damaged myself and all creation in the process.

Jesus' words in today's reading spell out this truth for us, using the example of the vine that will be fruitful only in its wholeness. The branch that is cut off will wither. The branch that remains on the vine will bear grapes, and those grapes will become "fruit that will last."

So, paradoxically, as we are being sent out, we are also being urged to remain connected to the vine. For me, this connectedness has to do with remaining in relationship with God through prayer and reflection, and remaining in relationship with the whole family of creation in a living web of interdependence and interrelatedness. This web is a bit like a vine, interwoven and intertwined. What happens to any part of it happens to the whole. What happens to the whole affects every part.

I remember a sunny summer morning in the vineyards of the Cognac region of France. I wandered up and down the lines of carefully tended vines, reflecting on what I had learned from the guide about the special conditions in this place that made it possible to grow the finest grapes for the production of vintage cognac. The ground here was stony, so the roots had to become strong in their thrust downward in search of water and nutrients. But the light had a special clarity that brought the grapes to the fullness of their flavor. This unique combination of harsh ground and gentle light reminded me of the action of God, the vinedresser, who also plants us in a place that will challenge our growth and at the same time provide the light of God's love. The result is fruit that will be distilled into something utterly distinctive—but only if we stay connected!

At the end of each line of vines was a little rosebush. At first I thought it was just a delightful decorative touch, but not so. The rose was there as an early warning system of any impending disease that might threaten the vines. If the rose began to die, urgent attention was needed by the vinedresser to protect the vines from the invading organism. The love of the vinedresser, I realized, goes far beyond simply providing the right conditions for growth and the right degree of necessary pruning. God's love goes so far as to give us God's Son who, like the rose, surrenders to death so that we might live.

And so we are challenged and loved, pruned and protected. The only thing God cannot and will not protect us against is our own desire for autonomy. If we choose to go it alone and try to live in our own strength, there will be no fruit. If we allow our "part" to remain connected to the wholeness of God's love and the world's needs, we will bear fruit worthy of the label "VSOP Special Reserve."

> ### *"Those who abide in me and I in them*
> ### *bear much fruit."*

Have there been times in your life when you have tried to go it alone, trusting in your own strength, without quality time with God and without too much concern as to how your actions and decisions might be affecting others? Don't judge yourself, but just allow any memories of times like these to surface in your prayer, noticing the effects of them.

Now recall the times when you have remained connected to the wholeness of God and God's creation—perhaps by making time for prayer and for service of others or making an effort to build real community. What fruits grew from those times?

Lord, the creative power we need comes from the wholeness of being in you, not in the partialness of our own little kingdoms. Please give us the grace to remain rooted in the soil, and not to be tempted by the fleeting attractions of our own little vases. Amen.

Sending

Read John 20:19-21; Isaiah 6:8; and 2 Corinthians 3:3.

The Christmas postal rush is over, and the staff in the sorting offices and on the delivery rounds are enjoying a welcome lull. But the excitement of seeing an unusually large pile of envelopes on the mat each morning is over too, until next year. I still have a childlike delight in waiting for the mail to arrive, whatever the time of year. Many a morning I listen for the sound of the mail carrier's footsteps crunching down the path, the clatter of the letter box, and the plop of the mail onto the hall floor. Then comes the ritual of discovery. The size and color of the envelope, the postmark, the handwriting, all add their own clues about the nature of what has been sent to me. Sometimes the crop yields nothing but bills and junk mail, and I retreat to my desk, vaguely disappointed. On other mornings there is real writing on the envelopes, and I know I have been sent a personal communication. I make myself a cup of coffee and sit down to savor the contents.

So I especially love Paul's analogy of our lives as "a letter of Christ." I wonder sometimes what kind of a letter I am going to be today, to those to whom I am sent, or on whose "mats" I arrive, invited or otherwise. Will my presence in their lives today be irksome, like a bill, or irritating, like an advertising circular? Will it be demanding, like a tax return, or will it be a churlish complaint about something or other, leaving the recipient feeling diminished and distressed? Or will my arrival in the lives of other persons today be invigorating and encouraging? Will it tell them something new about life that perhaps they are longing to hear but hardly dare to believe in? Will it make them laugh? Will it lift their hearts? Will it make them feel more alive than they did before?

And will Christ send me a letter today? Will someone cross my path who has something to show me about God's love and compassion, God's power or tenderness or challenge? Will I recognize God's handwriting in that person's presence?

We are letters from Christ, Paul tells us, written not with ink but with the Holy Spirit—that same Holy Spirit that Jesus breathes into his friends in the upper room, where they are cowering in fear of the authorities, and whence he sends them out to carry his truth and his life to the world. Christ no longer writes his letters on tablets of stone, like the ancient law of Moses, but on the tablets of human hearts. He writes upon our hearts in the quiet of prayer. Like the prophet Isaiah, we feel the touch of Christ's Spirit upon our hearts in a personal calling: "Whom shall I send? Who will allow his or her life to become a letter of my love?" And Christ leaves us free to make our response—yes or no.

To say with Isaiah, "Here I am; send me!" is to give the Lord permission to write divine communication into the fabric of our own daily living. God does this most effectively when we offer God a blank page that hasn't already been half filled with our own wisdom. God's handwriting will be most clearly legible if we respond to the promptings of the Holy Spirit, moment by moment, as God writes. God's message will be received without interference if everything we say is spoken in the spirit of God's love.

We are sent out as carriers of the good news that God's love is more powerful than the sum total of all the evil the world can come up with. All we are asked to do is allow God to write that message in our hearts and send us where God will. We usually won't know in advance the address to which we are being sent.

All that is asked of us, when God sets the divine seal upon us, is to respond with our own "Send me!"

"You are a letter of Christ."

Today, when you awoke, Christ "mailed" you into the world of this morning. He had something unique and special to say to someone about the nature of his love, and he could only say it through you. Look back over the day. Can you see what kind of letter Christ has written in your life today? Did you deliver it faithfully? Did you receive any letters from God yourself today? If so, give thanks quietly in your heart for the Sender, and for the person who delivered God's word to you today.

Lord, let the writing on my "letter" today be clearly yours and not my own, so that those who receive it may readily recognize the Sender's love. Amen.

Returning

Read Matthew 2:1-12.

God, so we are sometimes reminded, writes straight with crooked lines. We have no way of knowing the contours of the journey the Magi made in search of the mystery of God coming to birth on earth. We are told only that they misjudged their destination, trusting their own assumptions that a king would be found in a royal palace. This error of judgment was to cost them dearly and result, indirectly, in the carnage at Bethlehem when Herod's wrath was vented upon the infants and toddlers of the town. Other than that, we know only that they began their journey somewhere in the east where they first saw the star, and that after they had found the child Jesus, they returned to their homes "by another road." God's ways are not our ways, but they frequently lead us through our own convolutions and beyond our own obstacles, not only to discover the truth we seek but to return home enlivened by that truth and called to make it incarnate in our lives.

I was reminded of this tortuous way of doing things recently while watching a natural history program on television. I was riveted to the TV set, watching the amazing beauty of the coral reefs and the fish that inhabit them. But one fish caught my attention especially—the parrot fish.

Like all God's creatures, including ourselves, the parrot fish roams the created world looking for its heart's desire. For the fish, this comes in the form of the algae on the reefs. For us, perhaps, our desires would be less tangible. For the Magi, their great desire was to find the child whose star had guided them from the east, in search of something—or Someone—they could scarcely give a name to, yet whose birth would turn history around and upturn all their expectations.

In the film I was watching, the parrot fish found its meal of algae. But because this particular fish has enormously powerful jaws, it bites off whole lumps of coral reef and of solid rock along with its food. It eats the crockery and the cutlery along with the meal.

A mouthful of rock isn't what most of us include in our wish list of deep desires. But if you look back over your own story, how often has the search for your dreams and ideals cost you a few metaphorical broken teeth, as you have bitten on the hard rock concealed under some of life's most attractive surfaces? Failed love, broken relationships, redundancy where a career had been dreamed of, sickness and incapacity that drained the energy of life. For the Magi, the hard rock came in their encounter with Herod. On the surface, his words were a polite request to be kept informed. Underneath was the cruel rock of a tyrant's destructive intentions. The desire to find the Lord came along with the bitter ingredient of human brutality.

But the coral reef has not yet finished yielding up its secret. The parrot fish swallows the rock along with the algae, and in due course the rock is excreted again as fine white sand. The fine white sand gathers itself into coral islands—the kind of island that those who can afford it pay thousands of dollars to visit. (I don't suppose the glossy brochures tell would-be visitors exactly where the perfect sand of their dreams comes from!) Eventually seeds arrive, trees grow, birds colonize the islands, and animal life evolves. A whole new form of creation has come into being, just because the parrot fish swallowed some rock with its meal.

A similar circular route seems to describe the journey of the Magi to Bethlehem and back. They follow their dreams, just as the fish pursues its algae. They bite on the hard rock. But their return journey is the beginning of a whole new way of being human. They bring the good news of Bethlehem to the Gentiles, and we celebrate this breakthrough especially at the feast of the Epiphany. A new "island of faith" is born, taking a form no one could possibly have imagined. It will spread and grow, and we ourselves shall inhabit it. And it will always be a circular journey. Every new human life will make its own journey of discovery, in search of the "pearl of great price," and most of us will have to digest a fair bit of rock along the way. Yet all the while God is growing something amazingly new out of the wrecks we leave behind, whether deliberately, like Herod, or accidentally, as in the Magi's misjudgment of Herod and his strategies.

With these thoughts in mind, we might conclude our own journey through these pages by likewise returning to where we began—to the angel's words to Mary at the moment of Jesus' conception: "With God, all things are possible!" In God's hands, the worst we can do or experience can be reshaped and returned into the best we can imagine—and more!

"They left for their own country by another road."

Take a little time to bring your Advent journey to a close, perhaps by looking back over your whole life's journey. What star have you followed? What has been the dream that has inspired you, and the vision that has energized you the most? What have you been searching for? Do you feel you have found it? What "rocks" have you had to bite into along the way? With hindsight, can you see any "coral islands" that have evolved from those rocks? Has God brought something new into being out of the heart of your worst experiences—maybe a different way of seeing things, or a new depth of understanding or empathy?

Today, the feast of the Epiphany, is the beginning of God's mission to the whole of creation, far beyond the confines of the people of Israel. You are a part of that mission. Your life is a part of the new kingdom that God is bringing into being out of that mysterious mingling of our desires, our suffering, and God's love. Celebrate this "birthday" of God's kingdom-without-boundaries in your own way today, perhaps in the company of friends.

Lord, you have revealed your love to me. You have commissioned me to make that love a reality in your world. You have anointed me to serve your people and transformed my brokenness into a strand of your wholeness. You have freed me from the captivity of my own self-absorption, and you nourish my dreams with your own vision. Keep me rooted in you. Send me out with your seal upon my life. Return me to tomorrow's world, carrying the light of your mystery into every new beginning. Amen.

Journeying through Advent with a Small Group

PERHAPS YOU CAN MEET TOGETHER, through the weeks of Advent, with a small group of other Christians and use this book as a basis for your reflections and group gatherings. Sharing the journey in a small group is an excellent way to deepen our lives in God. Experience has shown that a few ground rules often help make such an encounter more fruitful.

Center the meetings around listening. Allow each participant to share whatever he or she feels comfortable sharing, arising from the reflections through the week. When a person has finished speaking, pause for a few moments of reverent silence to honor the sacredness of what has been shared. Avoid any temptation to solve one another's problems; to advise or direct one another; to fix things; or above all, to interrupt, criticize, or correct anyone. When everyone has had a chance to speak, you may wish to open up the meeting for persons to respond to one another or explore any issues further.

No one should ever feel pressured to share personal reactions and reflections with the group. *Let there be no coercion.* If a participant prefers to remain silent, receive that silence with respect and prayerful reverence.

Keep things simple. Focus the meeting on talking about the week's reflections, not on offering elaborate hospitality, which can distract from the simple sharing. You may want to encourage each participant to host the meetings, on a weekly rotation, so that each person takes a turn facilitating the group. Facilitating the group means, quite simply, ensuring that each person who wishes to share has an opportunity to do so within the given time constraints and without interruptions.

Allow the Holy Spirit to guide your meetings, and don't feel any compulsion to "follow the book." You may find it helpful to focus on just one of the points suggested at the end of each week or simply to share what the week has meant for each of you. This isn't a "course." What is offered in the text is intended only as a suggestion, not as a directive.

Refrain from judging yourself or anyone else in your reflecting or sharing. The Gospel urges us, "Do not judge," and this includes self-judgment. Focus on what has been life-giving and on what is leading you closer to God. Let God do the rest.

Above all, enjoy your meetings, remembering that Christ is present among you always.

WEEK 1
Theme: Looking for God's Guidance

PRAYER

Our hearts' deepest dream, Lord, is to make your dream incarnate in our world. Yet it is so often so hard to find our way through the maze of our circumstances. Please give us the grace to search for and find the signs that lead us to you, amid the confusion and ambiguity of our daily living.

SCRIPTURE

"Look, here is the Lamb of God!" (John 1:37).

REFLECTING

This week we have reflected on some of the many ways God reveals God's mystery within the ordinary events and encounters of every day. Sometimes these glimpses of guidance happen when we risk stepping out of our comfort zone, letting go of our illusions of control. Sometimes they occur when God breaks right through our carefully laid plans and intentions, and we suddenly realize we are in the presence of One infinitely greater than ourselves. Sometimes God seems to speak to us more clearly when we are at the end of our resources than when we think we have "gotten it all together." Sometimes God's leading seems to take us on a convoluted pathway when we think we could have found a shortcut, if left to our own devices. Sometimes it is tempting just to stay with the "received wisdom" and not take the risk of discovering God's very personal kind of guidance in our lives. And always, we have choices—we can choose the more life-giving way forward in any situation, but we are free to choose what does not lead to life.

In the light of your reflections this week, what memory comes to mind from your own experience of times when you indeed discovered God's guidance for the way ahead? How and when did this happen? How was the guidance revealed? How did you react to it? What did this experience teach you about where and how to seek God's guidance in the future?

As much as you feel comfortable doing so, share your memories and insights with the group, and receive, lovingly and in respectful silence, the memories and insights of other members of the group.

What concerns are present right now in your personal life for which you need God's guidance? Do any of this week's reflections help you come closer to that guidance? In the silence of your heart, bring this situation to God in prayer. Share it in the group only if you feel completely comfortable in doing so. Resist any temptation to give advice to others in their searching. Simply let each person's quest be open to God as you bring these issues into your group prayer.

Finally, what events in the world news this week made you long to know what God is asking us, the whole human family, to do next? Where does our world need God's guidance most urgently? Once again, resist the temptation to fix the problem, but bring your thoughts and reactions to the group, sharing them in group prayer. Is there anything at all that you, as an individual or a group, can do in practice to address these situations in the wider world?

CLOSING

End your gathering with a prayer that feels right for you, perhaps along these lines:

> Lord, we have brought before you the deep concerns of our own hearts, our personal lives, and our world. We continue to seek your guidance in all we do and say, and in every choice we make. Please give us the strength, wisdom, and courage to turn our prayer into action in the specific ways we have shared with one another and with you during our gathering today. Amen.

Before you disperse, offer one another some gesture of solidarity in the search for God's guidance, and of your friendship with one another and your shared love of God. For example, you might hold hands and share a moment's silence together.

WEEK 2
Theme: Learning to Trust

PRAYER

When you brought us into this world, Lord, you gave us a precious gift of trustfulness. We trusted the world that welcomed us, as well as the adults who cared for us. We trusted the entire process of living without even thinking about it. But like all our fellow human beings, we lost that deep trust. We have become people who easily fall prey to fear. We are suspicious and distrustful of people around us, especially those we do not know, those who speak a different language, or those who come from a different culture. We, and the world, urgently need to recover the gift of a trusting heart. We ask you, this week especially, for the grace to learn to trust in you, for when we trust in you with our whole hearts, we see all our lesser fears from a different and more healthy perspective.

SCRIPTURE

"Then Mary said, 'Here am I, the servant of the Lord; let it be with me according to your word'" (Luke 1:38).

REFLECTING

It's one thing to read a manual on cycling and know, in theory, exactly how to do it. It's quite another matter actually to get on the bike and ride it! During this second week of Advent, we have been reflecting on how we might grow in our willingness to trust God's guidance in our lives. On the surface, we are being asked to trust something that seems ephemeral and far from solid in the world's eyes. There are no insurance policies or guarantees. We are asked, over and over, to take the leap of faith into the unknown Mystery, trusting only in our experience of God-with-us. There is no certainty. Instead there is a call to surrender our own cleverness to a deeper wisdom. There are no complex contracts. Instead we are invited back into the simplicity of the present moment. Trust will not come from seizing the reins of circumstance and steering events in our own direction. Rather, it will be learned in obedience to the hidden imperatives of God within our hearts. We are asked to set out on an adventure, not to settle into a fail-safe system. We are invited to trust our dreams. The Incarnation is the living model of what happens when Jesus trusts God's dream so fully as to enter right into the heart of it and make it reality.

What memories come to mind of times when you have trusted God's action in your life so much that you were enabled to follow your dream? When has your trust faltered, and how was it renewed? Share whatever you can of these memories with the group.

Has there been any specific moment this week when you have been challenged to move forward in trust, without necessarily possessing all the relevant facts and forecasts? How did you react? Don't judge yourself. Simply to acknowledge the challenge is a courageous step forward along the path of trust.

As you reflect on world events, this week especially, where do you find evidence of trust and confidence between peoples? Where do you find a breakdown of trust? Where is fear most evident, and what are its effects? Every time you make a choice for love and in trust, you add a little drop of trustfulness to the ocean of humanity. What single action could you take personally right now to contribute to increased trust in your world? What could the group as a whole do to make the world or your immediate neighborhood a more trustworthy and less fearful place?

CLOSING

End your gathering with a prayer together for the issues that have been raised, perhaps along these lines:

> Lord, we know that fear paralyzes us, but trust frees us to move forward in renewed confidence. Yet our world is so dangerous, and our culture feeds on fear. We beg for your healing touch upon our own fear-filled hearts, so that we might go out in your name as carriers of light and trust, who, in however small a way, dispel something of the darkness of suspicion that envelops our world. Amen.

During your gathering you have made trust a reality by entrusting to one another something of the depths of your own hearts. Acknowledge and celebrate that act of trust for what it is, perhaps by offering one another a sign of peace and love.

WEEK 3
Theme: Where Does Wisdom Dwell?

PRAYER

> We believe, Lord, that something of your own infinite wisdom dwells within our own hearts. Our intuition tells us this, but so do all the spiritual traditions of our world. When you lived among us as a man two thousand years ago, you urged us always to seek the pearl of great price within our own hearts and our own life circumstances. And so we ask you this week for the grace to discover and nourish the seeds of divine wisdom you have planted in our hearts, and to let them bear fruit for our world.

SCRIPTURE

"Give your servant therefore an understanding mind, . . . able to discern between good and evil" (1 Kings 3:9).

REFLECTING

This week we have reflected on sources of wisdom that dwell in our own hearts and experience. We have thought about what it might mean to have a discerning heart, a heart that is tuned to discover and follow the more life-giving, the more loving, the more Christlike way in every situation. We have noticed that wisdom is like a plant whose seeds we carry but which requires slow growth and careful tending, and we also realized that suffering can often be a crucial experience that fosters the growth of wisdom.

As you reflect on these ideas, which readings particularly connected with your own experience? How did you react to the daily exercises? If anything helped you and you feel comfortable sharing, tell the group what helped you and how. How do you feel you have been led deeper into wisdom's gold mine, and how has this influenced your choices?

In what areas were you challenged to make specific choices this week? How did you decide what to do? With hindsight, how do you feel about your choice? What would you want to change if you were facing the same kind of choice again? Remember the golden rule: Make no judgments!

As you look back on times of struggle or suffering in your life, how do you think they led you to new growth in wisdom and understanding? In what ways do you feel these experiences led you closer to God?

In our world today, discerning any growth in wisdom and understanding can be difficult, and yet nothing, we believe, can ultimately subvert God's dream for creation. As you look around you, perhaps in the events that happened in the world this week or something you may have seen on television or read in the newspaper, can you see any sign of the seeds of divine wisdom beginning to germinate and grow? Share as many of your findings with the group as you can.

What actions can you take, either individually or as a group, to nourish wisdom in the world? Consider how you might make more prayerful discernments yourself, or how you might raise issues that need the light of God's wisdom (perhaps in informal conversation in your family, neighborhood, or the wider world).

When the pregnant Mary met the pregnant Elizabeth, the children in their wombs stirred in joyful recognition of each other. In each of us is a Christ, still unborn, but gestating. When we listen with our hearts to another's story, we will recognize the unborn Christ within that person, and our own hearts will stir in mutual recognition. In your own encounters with others, where have you noticed this heart reaction taking place? Can you trust that a seed of God's own self is coming to birth in you?

CLOSING

> *Lord, you nurture your divine wisdom in our hearts and our lives, and we thank you for this great blessing. Yet the way to birth is long and sometimes painful. Please give us the grace and courage to remain faithful to our calling to bring some fragment of you to birth in our world, something that only we, uniquely, can bring to birth. Bless the Christ we carry, and bring him to birth in our everyday living. Amen.*

Just as the unborn John greeted the unborn Jesus when their mothers met, so the unborn Christ within each of us leaps in loving recognition of the unborn Christ in other persons. Consider closing this week's gathering by greeting each group member in a way that consciously acknowledges the unborn Christ within that person. Knowing that each one carries the Christ child within his or her heart, make your response, perhaps by sharing a loving and reverent embrace.

WEEK 4
Theme: Journeying to Bethlehem

PRAYER

Lord, we believe that your coming to birth on planet Earth was not simply a historic event in a faraway time and place but the beginning of a process into which we are all called to grow into all that it means to be fully human. We know that this call will challenge us in ways we cannot and dare not imagine, and it may turn all our human wisdom upside down. Yet we long, above all, to play our part in this awesome process of becoming who we truly are. And so, today, we ask for the grace to enter into the heart of the Mystery of your birth.

SCRIPTURE

"And the Word became flesh and lived among us, and we have seen his glory, the glory as of a father's only son, full of grace and truth" (John 1:14).

REFLECTING

Since earliest childhood, most of us have grown up with the certainty that this week is the most magical week of the year. It is a week full of happy anticipation, leading to its climax on Christmas Eve and Christmas Morning, when for a few short hours the world seems to stand still. All work ceases (for most people at least), and the longing for peace reverberates around the world. Yet we know too that the magic has a shadow side. For the lonely, Christmas intensifies the isolation. For the unhappy, it deepens the pain. When tragedy strikes at Christmas, we feel the poignancy all the more sharply, and our hearts weep for those affected. To enter into the joy of the New Life means that we must also enter into the agony of bringing that Life into the world.

In what ways have you been able to enter into the mystery of Christmas this week? Which reflections spoke especially to your heart? What memories did they evoke for you?

Perhaps the week has pitched you into an ambivalent mix of happiness and sadness: the longing to belong, the struggle to create and maintain harmony in your home, the joy of those special surprises that astonished and delighted you—the unexpected gift, or the gesture of appreciation, or a time of stillness amid the storm. Share your experience with the group if you feel comfortable doing so. Don't be afraid to acknowledge the shadow side. Light and darkness are both partners in the birth-giving.

As you move toward the start of a new year, what can you, individually or as a group, do to bring something of the Christ-light into the lives of those around you in some practical way? Where might the "unwrapped" gift of the Christ child be present in your neighborhood, awaiting your visit? What might you bring to that twenty-first century Christ child?

CLOSING

Lord, if we enter into the light that surrounds your coming to birth, we will not remain unchanged. Tentatively, we step into your stable-home, hoping to hold you in our arms. Instead, it is you who takes us into your arms, and with a silent baby gaze, you challenge us to seek you in our sidewalks and tenements. Please give us the grace and the

courage to keep on saying "Yes!" long after the Christmas
season has passed. Amen.

End your gathering by making and expressing a special New
Year's wish for one another and for the group as a whole.

WEEK 5
Theme: Out into Another Year

PRAYER

Lord, our deep desire is to make space for your Spirit to
become incarnate in the circumstances of our own lives,
yet we know that this is not simply for our own sakes, but
for the love and service of all your creation. We have entered
into the mystery of your birth, each in our own way, and
now we ask you to send us out into another new year, to
carry the light of your love into a darkness that often
frightens and overwhelms us.

SCRIPTURE
"Peace be with you. As the Father has sent me, so I send you"
(John 20:21).

REFLECTING
God has God's own ways of preparing each one of us for the particular purpose for which God sends us out into the world at the
start of this new year. We have reflected on some of those ways
during this week's meditations.

Which of this week's reflections spoke to you especially? What
made them relevant to you? In what ways do they connect with
your own experience? Share your reactions with the group, if you
feel comfortable doing so.

What makes it possible for you to say, with Simeon, "My eyes have seen your salvation"? What experience in your own life has given you this kind of heart knowledge?

We read something in the passage from Luke that might be called Jesus' mission statement (see December 30). What does this mission statement mean to you personally—or to the group as a whole? If you were invited to write your own mission statement, what would you want to include in it? What would be most important to you?

Every day offers a new opportunity for God to send you out into the world as a "letter of Christ." What kind of letter have you been this week to the world and to people you encountered? When has God sent you "letters" in the form of other people? What kind of letters were they—letters of encouragement, affirmation, or challenge? How did you respond?

God's nature is always to be transforming—transforming our worst into better, our mediocre into good, and our good into best. How do you see the pattern of this transformation at work in your own life, in the life of your family or neighborhood, or in the group? How might you actively cooperate with it? Remember, God can make coral islands out of the rocks we swallow! God can build wholeness out of our brokenness.

CLOSING

Lord, we have journeyed together through this holy season of expectation, fulfillment, and challenge. We have claimed your promise that "where two or three are gathered" you are there among us. Give us the grace to trust in all that you have revealed to us, in our own prayer and reflection, and in what we have shared in the group. Commission us now to journey on in faith, hope, and love, toward everything that tomorrow holds for us, and for our world, knowing that

154

your Light can never be extinguished, even by the deepest
darkness, and that your Dream is the one unshakable reality
in our shifting lives. Into your hands we commit ourselves
and one another, now and forever. Amen.

You might like to end your gathering by devising a ceremony in which you commission one another to go forward in God's love and power. This can be simple and should reflect the spirit and imagination of the group and your desires for the future. For example, you might anoint one another with oil or offer a personal prayer for each person, expressing his or her special giftedness and dreams. Add music, songs, or readings (scriptural or otherwise). Arrange a celebration feast if you feel so inspired, perhaps a potluck meal.

About the Author

MARGARET SILF is an ecumenical Christian, committed to working across and beyond denominational divisions. She lives in North Staffordshire, England with her husband; they have one grown daughter. For most of her working life she was employed in the computer industry. In 2000 she left that industry to devote herself to writing and accompanying others on their spiritual journeys, especially on retreats.

Silf has written a number of books, including *Inner Compass: An Invitation to Ignatian Spirituality, Close to the Heart: A Practical Approach to Personal Prayer,* and *Going on Retreat: A Beginner's Guide to the Christian Retreat Experience* (Loyola Press); *Sacred Spaces: Stations on a Celtic Way* (Paraclete Press); *Wayfaring: A Gospel Journey into Life,* and *At Sea with God: A Self-Guided Spiritual Retreat* (Doubleday).

EVERY DAY
Find a Way

Join with Christians around the world who read and pray—every day.

The Upper Room is a daily devotional guide that unites nearly three million Christians around the world into a global Christian community.

If you are searching for ways to deepen your relationship with God, *The Upper Room* is the ideal devotional guide. It encourages Bible reading, prayer, and meditation—practices that help you grow in the faith. Each day's devotion offers a Bible verse, suggested Bible reading, prayer, prayer focus, and thought for the day. Plus, there's a discussion guide for small groups to use. It's the most versatile, economical resource available for church groups or daily devotional practice.

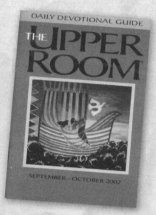

DAILY DEVOTIONAL GUIDE

THE **UPPER ROOM**

SEPTEMBER – OCTOBER 2002

To order individual subscriptions, call
1-800-925-6847

To order standing orders for groups, call
1-800-972-0433

Visit us online today!
www.upperroom.org

Other Advent Resources from Upper Room Books

Reflections of Messiah
Contemporary Advent Meditations Inspired by Handel
by Jim Melchiorre

Listening to Handel's oratorio *Messiah* and reading the scriptures on which Handel based his great work inspired journalist Jim Melchiorre to explore the message of *Messiah* for today's society. In so doing he came to fresh understanding of the radical and prophetic mission of Christ. Each meditation in this daily devotional guide includes a scripture verse, a powerful story about a contemporary person or event, a brief prayer, and reflection questions for individuals or groups.
ISBN 0-8358-9856-3 • 128 pages

Manger and Mystery
An Advent Adventure
by Marilyn Brown Oden

Recover the simplicity of the stable; rekindle the sacredness of the Advent season; remember the song of Mary; reclaim and follow the star. In *Manger and Mystery*, Marilyn Brown Oden invites readers to reflect on what the birth of the Christ child means to us today. Suitable for individual or group use, this Advent study beckons us to journey deeply through the season, wrapping time-worn customs in new expectations.
ISBN 0-8358-0861-0 • 128 pages

While We Wait
Living the Questions of Advent
by Mary Lou Redding

This Advent study resource for individuals and small groups offers readers new ways of connecting with their own faith questions. You'll have the chance to look at some biblical figures on whom we don't always focus during Advent. Tamar, Ruth, Mary, Elizabeth, Zechariah, and the Magi ask questions that resonate with contemporary Christians during this season. *While We Wait* gives readers unique perspectives on the events of Christmas, complete plans for small-group sessions, daily scripture reading and reflection questions, and introduction to the spiritual discipline of breath prayer.

ISBN 0-8358-0982-X • 136 pages